UNKNOWN TO HISTORY & FAME

A collection of prose, poetry and photographs from 19th century Walberton, West Sussex.

· BRENDA DIXON ·

WOODFIELD

ARUNDEL · SUSSEX · ENGLAND

First published in 1992 by
Woodfield Publishing
Woodfield House, Arundel Road
Fontwell, Arundel, West Sussex, UK

A Catalogue Record of this title
is held at the British Library

ISBN 1 873203 13 6

Printed in England

DEDICATED TO
DAVID AND MARJORIE HUMPHREY

All author's royalties from the sale of this book
will be donated to the Walberton Village Hall Fund.

Acknowledgements
West Sussex Gazette, Arundel
West Sussex Record Office, Chichester.
Chichester Public Library
Public Record Office, Kew.
The Reading Room, British Library, London
Lord Egremont, The Petworth House Archives

John Eyre, Walberton
John Booker, Walberton
Major Thomas, Fishbourne

With special thanks to Susan Millard, Chichester
and Elizabeth Thomson, Slindon.

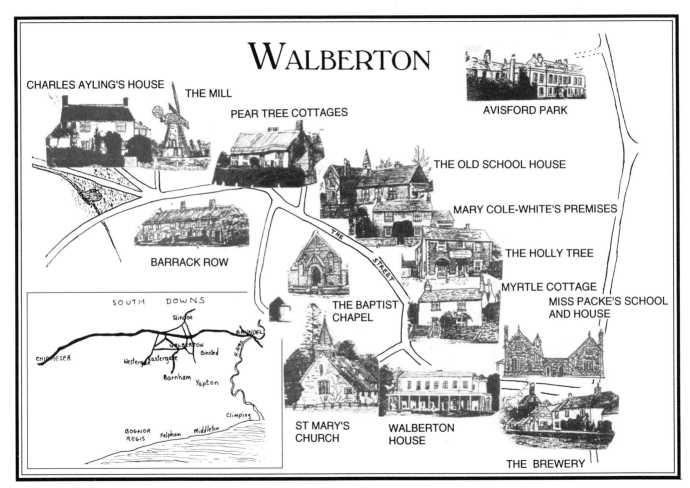

WALBERTON

CHARLES AYLING'S HOUSE

THE MILL

PEAR TREE COTTAGES

AVISFORD PARK

THE OLD SCHOOL HOUSE

MARY COLE-WHITE'S PREMISES

THE HOLLY TREE

BARRACK ROW

MYRTLE COTTAGE

MISS PACKE'S SCHOOL
AND HOUSE

THE BAPTIST
CHAPEL

SOUTH DOWNS

Slindon

ARUNDEL

CHICHESTER

WALBERTON

Binsted

Westergate   Eastergate

R. Arun

Barnham

Yapton

Climping

BOGNOR
REGIS   Felpham   Middleton

ST MARY'S
CHURCH

WALBERTON
HOUSE

THE BREWERY

· BRENDA DIXON ·

CONTENTS

INTRODUCTION

"Our village is a spot unknown to history and fame
The page of high heroic deeds has never held its name."

These lines are taken from a poem by Walberton writer Charles Ayling whose many poems and articles for the *West Sussex Gazette,* dating from 1856, were the inspiration for this book. He was also a photographer – and from his few surviving photographs and those taken by Edward Humphrey, fragments of Victorian village life can be seen.

I have tried to assemble these fragments into a picture of Walberton and its inhabitants in the context of what was happening in England at large during the nineteenth century.

Information has also been collected from many other sources, including extracts from *The Walberton Almanack and Parish Register* which the Reverend Irvine, a Vicar of Walberton started in 1877. In this little magazine he always included a letter about the past year and information on such diverse subjects as the church, education, vaccination, the lending library and many other topics of village interest.

This introduction would be incomplete, however, without further reference to Charles Ayling...

He was the youngest son of William and Mary Ayling, who already had five sons and three daughters. According to the 1851 Census returns he was a schoolmaster of twenty-five years and lived with his father, a widower of seventy whose occupation was that of bricklayer and maltster. Harriet Saxby, a grand-daughter of thirteen and a house-servant lived with them at the Green.

By the 1881 Census he was shown as living at the Green, but by now he lived alone and his occupation was 'photographer'.

Glimpses of his childhood can be found in his writings.

I never was educated – never attended school six months in my life. My mother taught me to read and I read everything that came in my way – which was very little for books were not so cheap. Matters, needless to mention, would not permit me to attend our village school except at brief uncertain intervals. At nine years of age I was sent to Brighton to try the effect of change and as Brighton brightened me up, it was thought advisable to give me some little education there. A 'School for a Select Number of Boys' was selected. It may have been a good one but I attended that school two days and a fraction. The first day I was a looker-on. The second day I was put through my paces in reading, orthography, and so on and came off with flying colours. On the third day writing lessons came on, this was my weak side, the master inspected my work and called the other boys – twenty of them – and handed my book for general criticism. The result, the laughter and derisive remarks was too much for my boyish nature. Snatching the book from one of them, I dashed it into the pedagogue's face and ran out of the school. Nothing could ever induce me to enter school again. Some months after this I left my relatives and went home to my parents, and when about twelve years old I was called upon to

· BRENDA DIXON ·

work - to learn my fathers business - the art and mystery of laying bricks. For about five years I did the best I could, and then I ran away, back to Brighton, There I obtained employment and took steps to rectify my ignorance. A friend gave me lessons in music, Latin and mathematics and several other things besides, were essayed by unaided effort. Of course I did nothing well, but I was young and without a guide, and for a while I indulged the pleasant dream that a pleasant future lay before me, Then the accident of an hour laid all my castle building to dust and the greater part of the next seven years was spent in almost helpless weakness, but if ever I was educated my education took place then, With no money and few books, and fewer friends, the task was not very efficiently accomplished. With some pleasant exceptions I have found the world to be in the gross neither a kindly nor a truthful world.

A few more words about myself. I am a genuine Sussex simpleton and as such I have something to boast of in these travelling times. Though I have stood on the verge of our three adjacent counties, Kent, Surrey, and Hants, I have never set foot outside of Sussex. I have often wished to have just one look at London, But travelling is inconvenient with empty pockets.

Other glimpses of his life will be seen throughout this book. When he wrote the following he was a sad old man, but as will be shown, he lived to find he had more friends than he realised.

For many months past, through some affection of the sight writing has been a difficult and painful effort. Now it is too evident that nothing but a period of perfect rest for the visual organs can avert a calamity, the greatest that could befall one whose only pleasures for years past have been those of the book and pen. Both must be laid aside. I have borne much, and suffered much, and borne it, I hope, bravely and cheerfully, well nigh without friends, and without sympathy. For in a country village, if you have no money you have no good in you, and if you are poor and friendless you are a fair mark for every ill-natured, evil tongue. My slight connection with the West Sussex Gazzette has been a somewhat protracted one, and a hundred pleasant proofs have been shown me that beyond the range of an ungenerous unreasoning local prejudice my little efforts have been read with interest and pleasure. Possibly it is all over now, but the future is in other higher hands, and my future must be as God wills it.

Following the above article on 5th January 1889, A.C. Simoon of Hastings wrote to the *WSG* suggesting an Ayling Fund be set up as for more than twenty years the columns of the paper had 'been graced by the charming lyrics and graceful prose composition, and a free will offering of this kind would do much to lighten the darkness of that anticipated day.'

Charles Ayling obviously had many admirers, for contributions came from all over Sussex and further afield. A concert was arranged at the New Assembly Rooms in Worthing which realized £18.15.0, and another concert was to be held at Arundel. The fund was closed when the amount raised reached £75.19.10. Out of 136 individuals, small groups and entertainments, only eight people from Walberton contributed to this fund, but Lady Anson of Walberton and her friends were very generous.

In addition to this amount some £5 has been sent privately to Mr Ayling, and the kindness of Lady Anson and other friends has to be cordially acknowledged, Lady Anson has defrayed the cost of very comfortable apartments overlooking the sea at Bognor, where the aged poet finds himself looked after with great care. As well as neuralgia of the optic nerve he suffers from a spinal injury sustained through a terrible accident as a young man. We at the *West Sussex Gazette* like others little dreamt of the real facts. Mr Ayling, preferred to starve rather than drop a hint to anybody that his affliction had left him in recent years a legacy of poverty. The chronic invalid who often lay with little in the cupboard and raked by pain, has at last seen the milk of human kindness come to the succour of even a poor old poet who lived a solitary life in an isolated village.

Mr Ayling's income had in those years consisted only of an annuity of £20, which had been provided by a visitor staying at Slindon, who admired his poetry.

In his will he requested that a stone to the memory of his father, mother and sister be erected as he had been too poor for this to be done when they died, and a stone over his grave with:

"*In memory of 'A' who lived and died,*"

with a reference to Isiah Chapter 40 verses 6-8.

The voice said, Cry. And he said, What shall I cry?
All flesh is grass, and all the goodliness thereof is as the
*   flower of the field:*

The grass withereth, the flower fadeth: because the spirit of
*   the LORD bloweth upon it: surely the people is grass.*
The grass withereth, the flower fadeth: but the word of our
*   God shall stand for ever.*

He asked that if any money remained after these expenses it should go to charities in West Sussex.

This poem is full of sadness – particularly when one recalls that he wrote it on 30th December 1858, but lived for a further thirty-six years.

This is our village dormitory: here
Its toilers come, when weary of the day
Which seems so long to many - ending still
To soon for most, unwilling to be free
From labour's shackles; but how well they sleep
Without a sigh to ruffle their repose.
O, would that I were like them: I am tired

Of lifes dull journey, for the way is long,
And sad, and tedious, and the pleasant flowers
That grew in either hedgerow once, are gone -
All save one bright blossom, lingering still

'Mid the rough briars of entangling wrong
And bitter herbs and poisonous weeds, alone.
This is our village dormitory: here
Its congregating myriads sleep away
The height of life, and wait the coming morn.

· BRENDA DIXON ·

Charles Ayling's house,
The Green, Walberton.

Charles Ayling's headstone,
Walberton churchyard.

Edward Humphrey in his Draper's shop.

SETTING THE SCENE
The Village Green & Pond

SETTING THE SCENE
The Village Green & Pond

South of the downs between Chichester and Arundel, situated on the coastal plain, is the large West Sussex village of Walberton. Although today it may not be described as picturesque in the same sense as many a small downland village, it has its own distinct character, having a pond and a pleasant contrasting blend of old and new buildings, as it did in the nineteenth century.

The map (page iv), along with the population figures, shows the location and size of Walberton in the 19th century. As can be seen, Walberton is a fairly long village with houses mainly on 'The Street', with concentrations of houses near the church and round the village green and pond.

At the first census in 1801, 502 people were recorded as living in the parish. There was an increase in the population and by 1821 a peak of 687 had been reached; this was during a period when national figures also showed a considerable increase. Numbers had fallen to 561 by 1841 and this movement away from the village was partly due to emigration which is explained and described in its own chapter. After this there was a slow increase – and by 1881 there were 607 inhabitants. This figure remained fairly constant – in the low 600s – until the end of the century.

The village green and pond area was a busy part of Walberton, and an interesting picture can be obtained from Charles Ayling's writings and Edward Humphrey's photographs. The following two poems give a delightful contrast, one describing the pond in the winter of 1857 and the other the village green in summer.

The old familiar sheep-pond, that skirts our village green,
Brings mingled memories back today, of many a joyous scene;
For the spirit of the frost again, with petrifying hand,
Has touch'd the waters, and at once they emulate the land.

One day, I well remember how bitter cold it was,
The frost work pavement o'er the pond was clear and smooth as glass,
But then it looked as brittle too; while just escaped from school,
We met in earnest council round the margin of the pool.

Full many an eager, doubtful glance to the farther bank was thrown,
Each deemed his fellow's safety sure, but would not risk his own.
One's chilblains were so tender, one had cross-nails in his shoe.
One wished he had not been so stout - the slenderest of the crew.

Resolved at length to test its strength, and not to die alone,
I took a young companion's hand, which trembled like my own;
We boldly struck the slippery path, of course to find it fail,
The shallow waters could not drown, - or I'd not told the tale.

Well drenched, and pale with cold and fright, and rueful thoughts of
*   home,*
We boldly struggled through the ice as shipwrecked sailors through the
*   foam*
Our playmates welcomed us as men escaping from a storm
And then we hastened home to find a welcome much too warm.

Here we'll sketch our village green
A very special rural scene
With that lame donkey's frequent song
The windmill's rattling, clattering noise,
Those squalling girls, and quarrelling boys:
And then the whirling, dashing, splashing,
Of twice ten thousand sheep awashing,
Mother and lamb alike despairing.
And dogs abarking, shepherds sweering:-
It really forms in fullest measure
A scene of every thing but pleasure.''

The pond was called the 'sheepwash' by the villagers, as every year the farmers would bring their flocks for washing. Hurdles were set up as folds, and water drawn from the pond for the washing. In 1871 this article was written about the annual custom of sheep washing.

It is quite an ancient custom with us extending we believe, far back beyond the memory of anyone now living. For about two months in every spring the operation is carried on nearly every day. The pond being well adapted to the purpose, sheep are brought from most of the adjoining villages, and in the course of a season a good many thousands have to swim across the pond, after a preliminary scrub in the washers hands, In fact, with sheep so plentiful, one cannot help wondering why legs of mutton should be so scarce and so dear. It is curious to observe how uniformly they behave on reaching dry ground. Some have the fleece so wet they are unable to stand, but as soon as they regain their legs they give first the head and then the fleece a good shake, and quietly begin nibbling the grass. Now and then however, one will find its strength unequal to the task, and after turning round once or twice in the water will sink to the bottom; then the shepherd has to run in and drag it ashore, perhaps so nearly dead that they kill it on the spot 'to save its life'. It must be a cold, unpleasant operation for those engaged in it especially for 'Tom' in his tub (He was the sheep washer).

Imagine the children's delight and surprise when one morning in 1888 this scene occurred, presumably when a travelling circus passed through the village.

"I say look y'ee there," young Walberton cried out one morning with wonder in his tone at a spectacle once novel and interesting. It was nothing less than a troop of elephants and camels drinking and disporting themselves in our little sheep pond. There were five elephants and five camels. It was amusing to see the elephants twisting their trunks and pouring the water into their big mouths, and then spurting it over their shoulders in genuine story-book fashion. The illustrious visitors appeared to be very thirsty and they perceptibly lowered the level of the water by the quantity they took away inside of them.

From time to time, the Green was the scene of sporting activities such as impromptu cricket games and even boxing matches.

Young, or perhaps we should say, adolescent Walberton, has been taking lessons in boxing. They were obliging enough to pitch their booth close to our gate. There was a strong light inside, and so without going out of doors we could see the performance in the shape of silhouettes - shadows on the canvas of the tent. We could see the active idiots scuffing each other's ears and tumbling over each other on the ground. And we saw something else. Our village ladies, of course, were too modest to go inside, and much too curious not to wish to know what was going on. And so we saw certain feminine figures - full grown ones, too - creeping round the outside of the booth, peeping through slits in the canvas; while doubtless their gentle, tender bosoms throbbed with delicious horror as they saw the manly forms of the manly fellows knocking each other about. During the three evenings the 'boxing' was going on there was no reason for anyone to find fault. The whole affair was remarkably quiet, but the green presented on Sunday was not by any means creditable.

The Green, in wet weather, becomes water-logged and in the 19th century this area must at times have been virtually impassable as suggested by the following lines written on March 14th 1867.

The village green was a spot seldom heard of, and still more seldom seen by strangers, until the opening of the station at Barnham Junction. Since then I fear it must have seemed a name of ill repute among those, at all events, who have to cross it on foot - a somewhat numerous class. I am sadly sure our Slindon neighbours must at times apply some very ugly epithets to the choice selection of water, slush, and slippery mud which, in wet weather, is all we have to offer them, Surely a narrow footpath might be thrown up with little trouble and at very trifling expense. I know that many a pair of cold damp feet must have gone from the green to the station, and from the station perhaps many miles away, and who will tell with what deplorable results?

In very dry summers there was often a scarcity of water in the downlands and the villagers would come to Walberton pond for this very necessary commodity.

The heavy rains of the last few days must have been very welcome, for water was getting scarce in the village where it is not often a scarce article. In the 'hill' countries above us matters must have been very awkward. Water carts came from all directions, and in such numbers that sometimes they had to wait each other's convenience, the pond not being large enough to receive them all. There was a perceptible shrinkage in the volume of water every evening, but it recouped itself, in the course of the night. Village tradition says the spring, starting the stream which supplies the pond was never known to fail, and in a season such as this the pond has proved itself a public benefactor.

Charles Ayling often mentions the sad state of the Green on Sundays and below is one of his accounts.

Our village green recently presented a picture not by any means creditable to an English village on a Sunday afternoon. The green is somewhat triangular in shape - only it has more than three angles. One end of it suggested a country fair, with the tramping vans standing about, and behind those vans there was a line of not very white linen hung out to dry, and fluttering in the wind, while the women and children loitered about in all sorts of attitudes, except the picturesque or the pleasant. On the south side the men were holding a miniature horse fair, chaffering over the animals, and showing off their paces in very horsy fashion. Near the east angle of the green our local branch of the Salvation Army were holding their usual al fresco service, singing, preaching, praying, in the loud and vigorous style pertaining to the great army of General Booth. Of course we don't include this in the ugly part of the picture. It was its one redeeming feature, for the tramps have become a great nuisance with their pilfering. The village green, instead of a place of pleasant recreation for the juveniles, has become simply a camping and grazing ground for tramps and their horses.

The house that Charles Ayling lived in is on the left of the picture. The sails and fantail of the windmill can just be seen in the distance.

· BRENDA DIXON ·

Walberton House & Avisford Park

WALBERTON PARK AND AVISFORD PARK

Most villagers, including the farmers, rented their houses and land from the owners of Walberton Park or Avisford Park. Their influence was particularly felt during the first part of the century, but gradually diminished — especially during periods when these houses were left unoccupied or in the hands of tenants. Cottages, farms and land were occasionally sold, until eventually the large estates were disposed of in smaller lots.

WALBERTON PARK

In the early 19th century General John Whyte lived at Walberton Park and while Charles Ayling was a boy he heard how the Prince Regent (later George IV) visited the village.

The whole village and the villages for miles around, assembled to welcome the Prince and his companion, Mrs Fitzherbert. In the course of the afternoon they held a sort of 'levee' on the lawn, where the girls of the village made an offering of flowers to the affectionate and illustrious pair. When, late in the day, he drove off on his return to Brighton, the crowd gave him a cheer such as was never heard before nor since. Then to prove the sincerity if its loyal feelings, 'all Walberton got drunk at the General's expense'.

SUSSEX,

Within an easy drive of ARUNDEL *and* GOODWOOD,

Two miles from BARNHAM JUNCTION RAILWAY STATION, on the Main Portsmouth Line of the L. B. & S. C. Railway, from whence London and all the principal South Coast Watering Places are easily accessible, and seven-and-a-half miles from the Cathedral Town of CHICHESTER.

Particulars, with Plan, Views and Conditions of Sale

OF THE VALUABLE

Freehold Residential Estate,

KNOWN AS

"WALBERTON PARK,"

COMPRISING

A FINE OLD MANSION,

KNOWN AS

"Walberton House,"

Standing well within the Park, containing Noble Entrance Hall, 4 Entertaining Rooms, Billiard Room, 17 Bed and Dressing Rooms, and excellent Domestic Offices. CAPITAL DETACHED STABLING for 11 Horses, Double Coach-house, and other convenient Outbuildings. Well-timbered and tastefully laid-out PLEASURE GROUNDS, and large productive KITCHEN GARDENS.

"THE DOWER HOUSE," Grounds and Meadow Lands.

TWO CONVENIENTLY SITUATED HOLDINGS,

Known as TODHURST and PIGEON HOUSE FARMS,

CONTAINING

320a. 2r. 17p. of rich Pasture and well cultivated Arable Land.

A WELL-PLACED HOLDING known as "CHOLLER FARM,"

WITH ABOUT

229 a. 1 r. 25 p. of Brook and Arable Land,

A COMPACT LITTLE PROPERTY, known as STREET FARM,

With about 61 a. 3 r. 14 p. of PASTURE AND ARABLE LAND, 20 COTTAGES, and several ENCLOSURES or MEADOW LAND, situate in the Village. The Area of the whole Estate being

642 A.   :   1 R.   :   26 P.

or thereabouts, and producing a Gross and estimated Rental of

£1,459 17s. per Annum.

Which will be Sold by Auction,

BY

MR. J. R. THORNTON

At the Mart, Tokenhouse Yard, E.C.,

On WEDNESDAY, the 11th of JUNE, 1902,

Walberton House

England was at war with France and the old General did his part to prepare for the expected enemy.

We have often listened to the story of the preparations made both to fight or to run away. The able bodied were all enroled either as Militia or Volunteers. Old men and boys were 'told off' as drivers, waggons and carts were numbered, and women and children all knew in what special vehicle to take their seats, to be driven with sheep and cattle over the hills at the first note of alarm. At that time every public house in the county rang with a curious rhyme, something to this effect.

Says Boney to Johnny "I'm coming to Dover"
Says Johnny to Boney, "Tis doubted by some"
"But what" says Boney "if I should come over?"
"Then, no doubt," says Johnny, "You'll be overcome."

His old soldier-servant declared that 'the General swore too much – he was the wickedest swearer ever heard'. The General seems to have been an Englishman of the old school – hospitable to a fault. In the item of ale alone his expenditure must have been something serious. The beer was divided into three classes, good, better, and best. The small beer cellar was open to all who had business on the premises; and to a good many, perhaps, who only fancied they had, and 'Old Knibbs the gardener, got drunk on it nearly every night'. In a certain meadow, when peace was proclaimed, a bullock was roasted whole, and washed down with such large draughts of ale that Walberton seems to have celebrated the return of peace in a drunken fight 'all round.' This must have been the premature

LIVESTOCK RETURNS 1801	
Fatting Oxen	-
Cows	32
Steers/Heifers	22
Colts	7
Sheep	562
Lambs	98
Hogs	124
Sows	29
Pigs	206
Riding horses	27
Waggons	25
Carts	40
Other carriers	8
Draft horses	67
Draft oxen	-
Windmills	2 grinding 20 sacks of grain in 24hrs.
Private ovens	56 baking 1640 galls of bread in 24hrs.
Bakers ovens	-

CROP RETURNS 1801	
Wheat	291 ¾ acres
Barley	139 ¼ acres
Oats	67 ¾ acres
Potatoes	1 acre
Peas	26 acres
Beans	nil
Turnips/rape	114¼ acres

With the threat of invasion from Napoleon, livestock and crop returns were made by John Stevens, Curate for the County Lieutenancy on 4th December 1801 (see left).

peace of Amiens, as it is said to have preceded another general jollification in the Jubilee year which, of course, was 1810. Old Walberton with tipsy loyalty, drank His Majesty's health.

In 1816, General Whyte's son inherited Walberton House on his father's death and sold it to Richard Prime, who had the house reconstructed by architect Sir Robert Smirk (architect of the British Museum) on the site of the Tudor Mansion.

Richard Prime, as a large land owner and magistrate, was involved with the 'Swing' disturbances. There is evidence of a great deal of poverty, (see Emigration & Transportation) in the 1830s and this contributed to these disturbances, involving low-waged agricultural labourers in the southern and eastern counties, although twenty others were affected.

The name for this movement came from letters fictitiously signed 'Swing'. These were sent to employers demanding improved wages and/or the destruction of agricultural machinery. If the employers didn't comply, their houses, barns or ricks would be fired and their machinery destroyed. These disturbances throughout England culminated in the hanging of nineteen men, imprisonment of 644 and transportation of 481.

Richard Prime wrote on 16th November 1830 to John Hawkins:*

I have had a visit from about 150 of the mob ... As to the question of opposing force to force – is it prudent and advisable with only 150 soldiers in a District or a county about 30 miles from East to West and as much north to south

to begin to use the sword? I am decidedly of the opinion it would be a proper error as while they are dispersing the men from Felpham you might have a similar insurrection at Pulborough or Petworth ... If they had been exasperated and taught by their superiors to draw blood, where would it end ... Mr Cosens thinks that there have been strangers amongst them for some days past disturbing their minds, and distributing papers.

This disturbance was reported in the *Sussex Weekly Advertiser* and *Hampshire Daily Telegraph* mentioning how an outhouse of Richard Prime's was fired. Charles Ayling writes about threatening papers to Richard Prime which were 'left about his premises' and also a local incident of an incendiary fire. At the time it was difficult to catch those responsible although the following describes an attempt to bring them to justice.

A London serial, in an article on 'Nicknames' lately referred to an amusing police case, which came off in this locality a good many years ago – a case in which Justice was for once most cleverly outwitted, and which, though a mere child at the time, I happen to remember well. More than a few of your readers in this neighbourhood will remember it also. It occurred in 1831-32, I am not certain which. At that time incendiary fires were by no means rare in Sussex, and one of those fires had taken place within the boundaries of our little neighbour, Binsted. All attempts to discover the guilty parties were fruitless; but several months after, a troop of Walbertonians, emigrants to Canada, on their way to the

* John Hawkins, FRS FGS, 1761-1841, a Cornish gentleman who in 1808 bought Bignor Park and in 1826 served as Sheriff of Sussex.

point of embarkation, fell into a dispute about the fire. One of these dropped words which indicated a knowledge of the culprit, and those words reached an ear for which they were not intended - the late Mr Prime - a gentleman, by the way, from whose magisterial hand an offender had little reason to hope for mercy, and still less for escape. I believe the whole party were already embarked, when a warrant arrived which compelled some of them to return: one as a criminal, others to give evidence against him. The trial came on at the next Assizes, one 'Waxy' having the bad luck to find himself in the dock as the suspected party. And by a most ingenious arrangement of fiction, and disarrangement of fact, and combination of names and nicknames, they carried their point. All that could be extracted from them was an unintelligent rigmarole, until the whole court, counsel, jury, and judge were fairly baffled and beaten by an impenetrable stupidity - assumed of couse. And so 'Waxy' with a very ugly case against him, escaped for want of evidence, and the whole party came home with flying colors, and of course most magnificently drunk, for teetotalism was not invented then. One of my luckless relatives was among them, and his amusing, hiccuping account of the trial so caught my fancy that, child as I was, it was never forgotten. Many great and and some pleasant changes have occurred in the village since that time, but I am not aware that our 'simple annals' record any similar attempt, or in fact, any very serious subsequent crime.

From the Streatfield Papers, a letter from Mrs Richard Prime, who was a member of that family, tells of the uncontested election and the reaction of the villagers.

June 28th 1847

Your account of Prime's success with his speech [to the farmers' protectionist meeting] at Brighton is very gratifying - and nothing can be more flattering than the fact that the papers of the other Party [free-traders] in endeavouring to find fault, speak of him as most respected and most sensible, honourable, talented etc, etc. - that in the enemy Camp is a testimony so worth merit I shall be heartily glad when all is over on Tuesday night. The enthusiasm in Walberton and neighbourhood is really very droll, the Parishioners want to take the horses from the carriage and draw the MP from the Green to his own door, but I have made a compromise with them and they will be content to march their band before the carriage from the Green - I believe half of them think they themselves will be MPs or derive some great credit from the Squire being one!!! . . . Wyndam, who is most truly friendly, lends Prime an apartment in Grosvenor Place 'till Easter - very considerate, is it not, and a saving of money as well as increased comfort.

However in contrast Charles Ayling describes Richard Prime as:

...a very influential personage and what ever may be the case lower down, he was very popular with his own class, that is the local Landocracy, which he represented in parliament for a few sessions. He was a Tory of the bluest and deepest tint, imbued with all the spirit and prejudice of downright honest old Toryism. One object of his aversion was the *West Sussex Gazette*. For years he would not let the paper enter his house

– not even the servants' hall. Of course it did, although we have seen the servants put it out of sight at the mere suspicion of his approach. Imagine the good gentleman's feelings when he found that one of his own villagers had dared to become a contributor. He never spoke to me again except once, and then we had a famous quarrel. I never could understand what the quarrel was about. In many villages we find those who exist only to curry favour at the great house or parsonage by retailing all the garbage of the neighbourhood. No sooner had they heard I was in disgrace with the great man that they poured into his ear every idle, ill-natured story, that falsehood could suggest. The result was very natural, and for me disastrous. Let it suffice to say that for two years, at least, not ten persons in the place would speak to me if I met them in the street. A game of falsehood and ill-feeling was started then which exists down to the present hour. In a little village community such mischief is never undone. Not one could give a commonsense reason for their ill-feeling, or any reason, except they have been the dupes of evil tongues which have poisoned a whole neighbourhood against me. At present my faults seem to have been dwindled down to these two: I don't go to church, and I still make use of my pen, which has never learned how to puff and flatter and belaud – not even to put money in my purse where there has always been plenty of room for it. In presuming to use my pen in the first instance I ventured one step out of the beaten path of village life and it has cost me dear.

When Richard Prime died in 1866, Walberton Park passed to Captain Arthur Prime whose only son Arthur Henry had died of consumption on board his yacht on the river Tagus, Portugal, in 1880.

John Maxwell, the farm Bailiff, wrote two letters to his daughter Jean about Captain Arthur Prime's death. The following are extracts from these letters where it was revealed when the Will was read that Captain Prime had been leading a secret life in London.

12th January 1883.
Poor Captain Prime is dead. He died on Wednesday evening about 7 o'clock. His death was expected. A week previously Dr Collins told them that he would not live much longer than a week and on Wednesday morning he told them he would not live 24 hours. Captain Prime is going to be buried on Tuesday at 1.30pm. I had to look out twelve bearers to carry him, and they all met here last night and were measured for a suit of black including hats, neckties and gloves. Two men came from Arundel to measure them. The bearers names are Barnes, Henshaw. Jack Leggett, Albert Leggett and his father, Harry Hatcher, Peskett, White, Moore (keeper), Ted Burch and Charles Westbrook. A dressmaker is also making dresses for Mrs Prime and the servants. I have also got measured for a suit of black. Sergent is making the coffins. There will be three coffins, first an oak coffin, then a lead coffin, and an outside polished oak one. I assisted to put him in his coffin this afternoon. On Monday he will be soldered down stairs and put in the polished oak coffin which will stand in the drawing room until Tuesday. In Captain Prime I have lost a good friend and employer. However, others may speak against

him. I have no reason to do so, I do not think he ever spoke a cross word to me all the 14 years that I have been with him. After the funeral the 'will' will be read, and then publicly known how things are going to be. I know pretty well already how things will be, I dare not tell it now.

Saturday night – We have been preparing the Vault for Tuesday. Sergent is still working at the outside coffin. He and his man and boy were working on it till 1 o'clock last night and says they will be working till 2 o'clock tomorrow morning before it is finished.

Sunday morning – I went upstairs and saw him this morning. He does not yet look much altered only thin and pinched.

17th January 1883

Well, poor Captain Prime was buried yesterday. He was carried out through the little gate into the Church Yard. The procession started from the colonnade. He was carried up into the chancel of the Church and from there to the vault.

Many of the neighbouring Gentry, the tenants and trades people followed him to the grave. There were hundreds of people in the Church and Church Yard. Your mother, all the children and Mrs Hatcher were there. There were many beautiful wreaths sent, so that the coffin was quite covered with flowers. After the funeral they all left the house. Mrs Prime gave me poor Captain Prime's gold watch and chain as a souvenir. I daresay you know that Captain had a woman in London who has five children. Well he has left the place to them. It will be in trustees hands, and let for 14 years, and after that they will come into it. I don't know how things are going to be, I have been told they must keep me on as they could not do without me, but we will talk the matter over when you come home.

Due to these circumstances, Walberton House was let, and while Lady Hood was a tenant she entertained the children in the grounds on the occasion of the Golden Jubilee of Queen Victoria in 1887.

The eventful day is over and gone, and it is pleasant to know that Walberton first, and then Arundel, and then Chichester and then all England, and then the whole British Empire, celebrated Her Majesty's Jubilee in very handsome style. On looking from the window we saw very brilliant bunting waving round our village Green, nearly all the flags appeared to come out of the chimneys. The great event of the day was the dinner of course. It came off in some large sheds, on what is called 'Dairy Farm,' near the Church, a very convenient, central spot. It appears to have been quite a stylish affair. Our villagers for once, almost without exception were transformed into 'gentlemen diners out' and with true village politeness and good breeding they took their ladies to dine with them. After dining, the party adjourned to one of Mr Booker's fields for sports and pastimes, and a little more drink. The juvenile party so kindly entertained by Lady Hood and her youthful family, in front of Walberton House, seem to have had a remarkably good time of it. It is a beautiful spot, and in such wonderful weather the scene must have been highly animating and interesting. The feast provided for them appears to have been on a very extensive, brilliant scale. Among other gifts each child received a handsome Jubilee Medal, which we hope they will long preserve in memory of a memorable occasion and a day of pleasant things.

WALBERTON PARK, SUSSEX.

General Summary.

DESCRIPTION.	TENANT.	ACREAGE. A.	R.	P.	RENT. £ s. d.	REMARKS.
Walberton House, Gardens, Stables, and Pleasure Grounds ...	In Hand	15	0	2	350 0 0	Estimated rent, including the shooting over the Estate.
Todhurst & Pigeon House Farms, and Five Cottages	Mr. W. H. Langmead	320	2	17	539 0 0	
Street Farm	Mr. W. Ewens...	61	3	14	72 10 0	
Choller Farm and Two Cottages..	Mr. F. G. Fleming	229	1	25	280 0 0	Divided into two lots for the purposes of this sale.
Meadow Land	Mr. G. Burch...	4	2	11	10 14 0	Tenant paying Tithe.
Ditto	Miss Bell	2	3	33	6 0 0	Ditto.
Walberton Green.....................	Mr. A. Bowly...	0	3	36	0 16 0	Ditto.
Park House, Gardens, Stables, and Meadow............................	In Hand	4	1	31	80 0 0	Estimated.
Pair of Cottages	Rev. W. P. Crawley	0	1	0	12 0 0	Tenant paying rates.
Range of Three Cottages	Messrs. White, Moore & Hughes	0	1	17	16 16 0	Ditto.
Cottage	Mr. West	0	0	17	9 0 0	Ditto.
Ditto	Mr. C. Mills...	0	0	22	12 0 0	Ditto.
Range of Six Cottages	Messrs. Barnes, Farernden, Baker Adlem, Stent & Tyrrell	0	3	14	36 19 0	Ditto.
Range of Four Cottages............	Messrs. Moulsey, Mills, Keats & Farrenden	0	2	3	16 0 0	Ditto.
Pair of Cottages	Messrs. Light & Westbrook	0	0	16	9 12 0	Ditto.
Cottage............................. ...	Mr. J. Humphrey	0	1	8	8 10 0	Ditto.
Total...... A.		642	1	26	£ 1459 17 0	

Arthur Prime, Captain, Dragoon Guards, D.L and J.P for Sussex. Died 10th January 1883, aged 63 years.

On the 11th June 1902 Walberton House was to be sold by auction and an insight into the house and grounds can be gained from the sales catalogue (see opposite).

Walberton House viewed from the south.

22ND JUNE. 1897.

𝔚alberton 𝔇iamond 𝔍ubilee 𝔖ports

PROGRAMME.

Commencing 3 p.m.

No.		First Prize.	Second Prize.	Third Prize.
1.	Throwing the Cricket Ball. Open.	Biscuit Box.	Butter Dish.	
2.	Ditto, for Boys under 16. ...	Writing Desk.	Games.	
3.	100 yards Race for Boys under 16 ...	Ink Stand. ...	Preserve Dish.	
4.	100 ,, ,, Girls ,, 17 ...	Work Box. ...	Writing Desk.	
5.	High Jump for Men. ...	Clock ...	Platter and Knife	
6.	Ditto, for Boys under 16 ...	Ink Stand ...	Clock	
7.	120 yards Hurdle Race. Open ...	Ink Stand ...	Clock	Preserve Dish
8.	100 yards ,, ,, ...	Ink Stand ...	Case of Razors	Clock
9.	Long Jump. Open ...	Case of Carvers	Butter Dish	
10.	Ditto, Boys under 16	Hanging Brushes	Purse	
11.	50 yards Sack Race. Open ...	Case of Carvers	Cruet ...	Hanging Brushes
12.	80 ,, Race for Women. Open ...	Quilt & table cloth	Case of Scissors	
13.	80 ,, ,, Girls under 17 ...	Work Box ...	Case of Scissors	
14.	Quarter Mile Race. Open	Case of Carvers	Case of Razors	Preserve Dish
15.	Ditto, for Boys under 16	Ink Stand ..	Case of Brushes	Purse
16.	100 yards Three-Legged Race. Open	Platter & knife (2)	Clock (2)	
17.	Tug of War, 12 a side. Men ...	Pocket Knives		
18.	50 yards Egg and Spoon Race for Women	Quilt & table cloth	Table Cloth	
19.	120 yards Consolation Race. Open ...	Biscuit Box ...	Platter and Knife	
20.	120 ,, ,, Women. Open ...	Hand Bag ...	Purse	

Judges.—Mr. W. Luxford, Mr. C. Coote, Mr. E. Booker.
Starters.—Mr. A. Booker, Mr. Ellis, Mr. S. Short.
Clerks of the Course.—Mr. J. P. Goodacre, Mr. J. H. Goodacre, Mr. Peskett.
Handicappers.—Mr. Tanner, Mr. E. Humphrey, Mr. Hatcher.

The names of those Parishioners intending to compete to be given to the Clerks of the Course not later than 2.30 p.m.

No winner to take more than two First Prizes or Three altogether.

All disputes to be referred to the Sports Committee at the conclusion of the Sports whose decision shall be final.

FIREWORKS 9.30.

J. W. MOORE, PRINTER, CHICHESTER.

Programme of events for Walberton's celebration of the Diamond Jubilee of Queen Victoria, 1897

THE AVISFORD PARK HOUSEHOLD, 1851

NAME	RELATIONSHIP	CONDITION	AGE	RANK OR PROFESSION	WHERE BORN
Eliza Louisa Reynell	head	widow	68	Marquese	Ireland, Dublin
A Landed Proprietor Farmer of 123 acres, employing 12 labourers.					
Amie Elizabeth Pack	daughter	unmarried	30		Devon, Plymouth
John Hamilton Lewis Anson	son in law	married	34	Baronet, JP Deputy	Marylebone
Elizabeth Catherine Anson	wife	married	29		Devon, Devonport
William Reynell Anson	grandson		7	Scholar at home	Sussex, Walberton
John Berresford Anson	grandson		6	Scholar at home	Sussex, Walberton
Lousia Elizabeth Ann Anson	grand-daughter		4	At home	Sussex, Walberton
Mary Louisa Anson	grand-daughter		2	At home	Marylebone
Elizabeth Georgiana Anson	grand-daughter		1	At home	Marylebone
Fredrick Arthur	Anson	grandson	4mth	At home	Marylebone
Elizabeth Hindshaw	servant	widow	65	Housekeeper	Cambridshire
Jane Davis	servant	unmarried	50	Cook	Glamorgan
Mary Graham	servant	unmarried	25	Lady's maid	Northumberland, Alnwick
Sarah Hoberoyd	servant	unmarried	37	Housemaid	Yorkshire, Dewsbury
Martha Herrington	servant	unmarried	22	Housemaid	Sussex, Boxgrove
Ann Booker	servant	unmarried	22	Kitchen maid	Sussex, Walberton
Frances Gramart	servant	unmarried	18	Scullery maid	Sussex, Slindon
William Murdoch	servant	unmarried	48	Butler	Scotland, Glasgow
John Barron	servant	unmarried	26	Bailiff – Farm	Scotland, Glasgow
John Star	servant	unmarried	35	Coachman	Sussex, Hastings
Joseph Badger	servant	married	30	Footman	Bucks., Marlow
Robert Barker	servant	unmarried	17	Groom	Sussex, Walberton
Mary Ann Minchin	servant	unmarried	28	Groomess	Middlesex, Hampton Wick
Ann Griffths	servant	unmarried	47	Nurse	Middlesex, Marylebone
Jane Brown	servant	unmarried	29	Lady maid	Middlesex, St.Pancras
Emma Wilkes	servant	married	33	Wet nurse	Surrey, Guildford
Emma Collins	servant	unmarried	17	Nursery maid	Cambridgeshire, Westley
Edward Matthews	servant	unmarried	31	Footman	Hants., Aldershot
Thomas Dilloway	servant	unmarried	20	Groom	Sussex, Northchapel

AVISFORD PARK

In 1835, Thomas Horsfield FSA described this mainly Georgian house as being situated "on an elevated site, tastefully adorned with sylvan beauty, and yet commanding extensive sea views."

At the beginning of the nineteenth century, Avisford Park belonged to Sir George Montague GCB, who was Commander in Chief at Portsmouth. On moving away from the area in 1811, he sold the house and 80 acres to Sir William Houston for £1,325.

Roman remains were found on the estate in 1817, when a farm-hand, whilst making a hole with a crow bar for the purpose of setting up a sheep pen, found it impossible to dig deeper than six inches. On taking a closer look he discovered a stone coffer. When the coffer was opened it revealed many items of pottery which were of a light red colour. These remains can still be seen in Worthing Museum.

In the early 1830s the Reynell–Pack family bought the house. The 1851 Census for Walberton gives an interesting insight into the composition of this household (see opposite).

The grounds of this house are charmingly pictured by Charles Ayling in his poem of 1873 called 'Avisford', and the layout of the house can be found from the sales catalogue of 1883.

It is a pleasant picture! shrubs and flowers,
Sequestered groves, and old ancestral elms,
Worn with the tempests of a hundred years.
Smooth - shaven lawn and cattle dotted park;
And sheep with piebald fleeces, black and grey,
And twisted horns and softly - pleading eyes.
Strangers they are and strangers-like they ask
A passing notice and the petting hand
Of gentle children - gentler ev'n than they.

It is a pleasant picture, Southward far
Where Arun runs to meet the restless sea,

The silvery waters sparkle in the sun
And light and shadow beautifully pay
O'er intervening acres stretching wide,
A noble sweep of glade and waving corn
All glistening for the harvest and for man.

Roman 'sepulchral antiquities' discovered at Avisford Hill in 1817.

Avisford House

· B R E N D A   D I X O N ·

ENTRANCE LODGE,

1883.

MESSRS FRERE, FORSTER, & CO.,
SOLICITORS,
28, LINCOLNS INN FIELDS.

MESSRS FAREBROTHER, ELLIS, CLARK & CO.,
SURVEYORS,
5 & 6, LANCASTER PLACE, STRAND, W.C.
AND 18, OLD BROAD ST, E.C.

T. MAY, LITH.

AVISFORD, IN THE COUNTY OF SUSSEX,

Five Miles from GOODWOOD, Three from ARUNDEL, Seven from CHICHESTER, Five from BOGNOR, and Five from LITTLEHAMPTON.

Two Miles and a half from BARNHAM JUNCTION and Three Miles and a half from FORD JUNCTION STATIONS on the L. B. and S. C. Railway, from whence London is reached in about Two Hours.

Particulars, Plans and Conditions of Sale

OF AN EXCEEDINGLY VALUABLE

FREEHOLD ESTATE,

SITUATE

IN THE PARISH OF WALBERTON,

AND IN THE HEART OF

One of the most Aristocratic Residential Localities in the South of England,

COMMANDING VARIED LANDSCAPE & MARINE VIEWS.

THE FINE

Old-fashioned Family Mansion,

STANDS IN A

GRANDLY TIMBERED PARK,

SURROUNDED BY WELL LAID OUT

PLEASURE GROUNDS OF ABOUT 7 ACRES,

Ornamented with exceptionally well grown Specimen Trees and Shrubs of luxuriant growth;

WALLED KITCHEN GARDENS WITH VINERIES & GLASS HOUSES,

EXCELLENT STABLING & DOMESTIC OFFICES OF EVERY DESCRIPTION.

THERE ARE ALSO SEVERAL

Residences, Dwelling Houses, Cottages, Shops and Accommodation Lands,

A WIND MILL, MILLER'S HOUSE AND HOMESTEAD, the whole occupying an Area of about

188 ACRES,

And constituting a most enjoyable but inexpensive Property for the Residence of a Country Gentleman.

Which will be Sold by Auction,

BY MESSRS.

FAREBROTHER, ELLIS, CLARK & CO.

At the Auction Mart, Tokenhouse Yard, near the Bank of England, E.C.,

On THURSDAY, the 9th day of AUGUST, 1883,

AT TWO O'CLOCK PRECISELY,—IN ONE OR MORE LOTS.

Pages from the sales catalogue of Avisford Park, 1883.

On Christmas Eve 1897 the Vicar William Irvine wrote for the *Walberton Almanack* a description of the events which took place to celebrate the Diamond Jubilee, held in June 1897 at Avisford Park.

What is true of all England, is certainly true of Walberton, viz. that all its events in 1897 have been entirely thrown into the shade by the one absorbing event of the Diamond Jubilee of the reign of our most gracious Queen.

As the day approached the several sub-committees who had undertaken the arrangements for band, dinner, sports etc brought their labours to a termination, and the treasurer downwards, could safely assert that he had done his duty. Thankfully we received a fine day. No one could have dreamed of a finer, and as 12 o'clock struck, the excellent band of Mr Blackman struck up, and the committee started their march from the east end of the village down to the Green. Then a halt for ten minutes, and then back to Mr Henty's new lodge. Then another halt, and then nearly all Walberton marched shoulder to shoulder to the great booth, where the gallant army commenced their attack (upon the viands, provided by Mr and Mrs Bennett, of the Balls Hut). The committee had a warm time of it carving, and many of the gentler sex were quite as active and useful in distributing the spoils. During the feast the band played, and then the sports began. The prizes were on the most liberal scale, and consisted of writing desks, work boxes, biscuit boxes, inkstands, clocks, cases of carvers, cases of razors, butter dishes, preserve dishes, hanging brushes quilts, table-cloths, bread platters and knives, hand bags, pocket knives, and purse; the cost of these reached £12..15..4, and they were purchased on very favourable terms by Mr E. Humphrey, who spared no trouble in his selection. 321 sat down to dinner – 232 of them as Mr Henty's guests; while Mrs Henty provided tea and medals for the children and entertained many of the adults with refreshments on the lawn, and 2/6 each to those unable through infirmity to be present.

Then came dancing to the excellent music of the band, and fireworks (another present of Mrs Henty's) and finally 'God Save the Queen,' and good night, between 10 and 11pm. The committee who superintended the sports were :- Messrs. Ellis, Short, Coote, A and E Booker, W Luxford, Tanner, J.P., J H Goodacre, Peskett, Hatcher, and E Humphrey, and they had a busy time of it and gave the fullest satisfaction to all parties. The total cost amounted to £78..8..2, Mr Henty kindly paying over £5 the deficit when everything was cleared off.

I cannot refrain from mentioning one incident: a few days before the festival, a message was sent to the Vicar from the Inspector of Police, offering the presence of a policeman; the Vicar's answer was 'No, thank you all the same, Walberton needed none in 1887, and can be trusted to behave equally well in 1897;' what happened proved that he was right, not a single case of excess or rough conduct was to be seen. The only disappointment in the day was caused by the enforced absence of Mr Henty who was engaged in military duties in Chichester (as Lt. Colonel of the Militia). In order, however, that he should be personally thanked for his generous help, some 200 of the villagers marched off to Avisford the next evening (Mr Henty having returned in the afternoon) and expressed through the Vicar their appreciation.

· B R E N D A D I X O N ·

Colonel Henty, owner of Avisford Park, was keen to protect his privacy and even went to the lengths of having this cottage demolished because it overlooked the Park from the opposite side of Yapton Lane (see picture overleaf).

· BRENDA DIXON ·

Emigration & Transportation

LIST OF NECESSARIES FOR EMIGRANTS TO UPPER CANADA

Families should take their
Bedding
Blankets
Sheets &c
Pewter Plates or Wooden Trenchers
Knives and Forks and Spoons
Metal Cups and Mugs
Tea Kettles and Saucepans
Working Tools of all descriptions
(A large tin Can or watering pot would be useful)

Single Men must have
A Bed or Matress
Metal Plate or Wooden Trencher
Some kind of Metal Cup or Mug
Knife, Fork and Spoon

All, or any of which may be procured at Portsmouth, if the Parties arrive there unprovided.

Besides various other portable Articles in domestic use (especially of metal) according as families may be provided. A Cask, not exceeding the size of a Hogshead or 60 Gallons affords an excellent and dry case for packing such articles as are not likely to be wanted 'till the end of the voyage. All packages should be marked with the owner}s name in Large Letters. One hundred weight of Luggage is allowed to be taken by each individual above 14 years of age.

The following is the lowest outfit recommended to Parishes for their Laborers

A Fur Cap
A warm Great Coat
A Flushing Jacket and Trowsers
A Duck Frock and Trowsers
A canvas Frock and two pairs of Trowsers

Two Jersey Frocks
Four Shirts
Four pairs Stockings
Three pairs Shoes
A Bible and Prayer Book

EMIGRATION AND TRANSPORTATION

The population of England and Wales had risen from nearly nine million in 1801 to double that by 1851, and had reached thirty two and a half million by 1901. Although since at least 1600 the population growth had been a constant source of concern, alarm did not set in until the early nineteenth century.

By 1650 many had emigrated to the New World and this continued over the years until, during the nineteenth century, due to the large numbers underemployed or unemployed, it was regarded as essential that many more should leave this country.

A committee was set up in 1826 to report to Parliament. Many people gave evidence to the committee including government officials from Canada; one suggested the land being good, "about 60,000 souls could be sent depending on

*This committee was started in 1832 under the Patronage of Lord Egremont. Attempts were made to persuade other Landowners to sponsor families from their Parishes. Richard Prime was one of those Landlords who took the opportunity of using this scheme and his motives for wishing to send many of Walberton's poor to America must have been influenced to some extent by the riots of 1830 when a mob of 150 paid him a visit and fired an outhouse. Further information on this can be found in the Chapter on Walberton House.

organisation". Several members of the House from Scotland gave evidence about redundancy of labour in Scotland and about possible removal, and a Police magistrate from London suggested that a system of "emigration of children for whom there is no other employment" could be provided. In this document it was stated that the evidence taken, "appears to establish the fact that in England this redundant population represses industry and sometimes endangers the peace of the Mother Country."

The subject of emigration was recommended to the House as one obvious and immediate measure for correcting in some degree this redundancy of population and for mitigating the evils which appeared to result from its existence. Such emigration should be voluntary and relate to the part of the community which might be considered to be in a state of permanent pauperism. It was suggested that legislative measures might be introduced to enable parishes in England to mortgage their poor rates for the purpose of forming a fund for the emigration of their poor.

Walberton had many permanent paupers, and evidence for this is seen in the 'poor relief' returns made in 1826 which recorded 147 permanent paupers and 86 casual. This represents 34% of the village. These returns did not show what sort of relief was given, but from the *Walberton Poor Book* for 1800--02 it appears that this was very varied. Many received clothing including stockings and shoes. Fuel and flour was distributed and there was also help with the rent, burials and illness, including the 'smallpox folks'. One family was inoculated at the cost of £4..4..0.

Between 1821--41 Walberton's population decreased by some 18%, mainly due to emigration. This is borne out by the Poor Law Union Papers for West Hampnett, where a letter to the poor law commissioners in December 1835 mentions the sum of money borrowed from Richard Prime of Walberton House towards the cost of sending emigrants.

In May 1932, 18 adults and 2 children were sent to Toronto in Upper Canada under the Management of the Petworth Emigration Committee,* the total expense of which was £280.

In March 1835 were sent to the same place under direction of the same committee 11 adults and 5 children, total expense £175..3..0.''

The Petworth Emigration Committee kept a minute book and from this it is known that nine of the passengers for the ship 'England' were from Walberton.

Two hundred and six passengers emigrated through this scheme on the ship *England* and reproduced opposite is the bill of fare allowed by the committee.

The 'tween decks of the *England* was divided into main and fore steerage, the former for females and the latter for single men and boys above 12 years of age. A water closet was placed at the after end of the main steerage on one side and a spare berth left on the other, to be used if required as a

Every person above 14 years of age — reckoning two for one under that age, and exclusive of infants, is entitled to receive, during the course of each week, the following rations, but to be given out at such times and in such proportions as shall be found convenient.

Meat	7lbs	or Meat	5lbs
Flour and Bread	7lbs	Bread and Flour	5lbs
Oatmeal	1lb	Oatmeal	1lb
Potatoes	4lbs	Potatoes	10lbs
Tea	2.oz	Cheese	1lb
or Coffee	¼lb	Butter or Lard	½lb
Sugar	1lb	Tea	2oz
Brandy, to those above		or Coffee	¼lb
14 yrs. only	½pt	Sugar	1lb
		Raisins	½lb
		Brandy, to those above	
		14 yrs only	½pt

Onions, soap, tobacco, vinegar &c in such quantities as may be directed by the superintendent.

Porter &c for the sick, under the direction of the surgeon.

The brandy to be given in not less than three times its quantity of water.

Provisions were put on board sufficient for 63 days or 9 weeks, and a ton of pure water for every four *passages*, which allows of 1 gallon per day, each *passage*, during the above named period.

Bill of Fare allowed by Petworth Emigration Committe

· BRENDA DIXON ·

hospital. Six feet by two feet was allowed per passenger for the sleeping berths. A surgeon was engaged to attend to the emigrants free of charge.

On Thursday 25 April 1833 the *England* sailed from Spithead with a fine easterly breeze and from the Log Book it is evident that many of the passengers suffered with seasickness at the start of the voyage.

> *Saturday 27 April.* Many people distraught with seasickness, brandy administered in pretty plentiful doses, sometimes mixed with laudanum as a soother.
> *Wednesday 1 May.* Wind increased to gales. Seasickness came on again. the women suffering the most. Hot coffee and brandy were given and porta (condensed) soup was tried. The men became troublesome. Supplied them with tobacco and brandy and the children with Gingerbread."

Before the emigrants left, the Petworth Committee wrote to Parish Officers recommending them to attend to the packing and to ensure the people were decently clad for their journey and to this end they provided a list of 'Necessaries for Emigrants to Upper Canada' (see opening page of this section).

In 1832 the printers J. Phillips of Petworth published *Letters and extracts of letters from settlers at the Swan River, and in the United States, to their friends in the Western part of Sussex.* Two letters were from emigrants from Walberton (*see* App. I). The first extract comes from Mark Ruel, who left his brother in Quebec, and the second from George Jordon who went to join his uncle and aunt at Pittesford, Monro County, New York.

From these letters the impression is given that once they had recovered from the journey they regarded themselves as being in a 'very fine country, plenty of everything that is needful both for body and soul.' They suggested that anyone going to North America should only bring shirts and cloth to make up after they arrive because: 'People wear their clothes different in this country: they wear no round frocks, nor breeches, they all wear coats and waistcoats like our English gentlemen.'

In the beginning of June 1870, Mr Booker, one of a party of emigrants who went out in the early thirties returned to see his family in Walberton, and in Ayling's article on this he states, 'Most of the party who went out with him, had they remained in England would have passed through life as farm labourers receiving ten or a dozen shillings a week. Now several of them are farmers themselves, prosperous and independent. Mr Booker considers Walberton has brightened up in externals since he saw it last.'

In another article he writes about some of the villagers who went away.

In those far away Thirties quite an emigration mania prevailed in our little village, when Walberton lost more than a tenth of its population. Not only isolated individuals, but large groups and whole families took wing for the West or the South. Among others, the mania seized my father's family and deprived him of more than half his children. One brother went to Australia, three others to Canada, and a sister to New York. A letter from this sister was about the passage made in a packet ship, bound first for Montreal to land passengers for Canada. As the ship sailed up the St Lawrence, cholera made its appearance and my sister's first experience on American soil was to find herself an inmate of the cholera hospital. The plague, so new and sudden, seems to have paralysed an almost disorganised society. I have since read accounts in print which have more than justified her letters. Crowds of sufferers were left to die almost without assistance, and when dead they were simply carted away in heaps and thrown into a common pit, my sister recovered and finally found herself in New York, about four months after date. There a warm welcome awaited her in the families of two paternal uncles settled in the States.

These were all emigrants to America but William Ayling, a bricklayer aged 25, undertook in 1836 the long and arduous journey to South Australia and Charles Ayling recalls his departure.

We can just remember the time when an elder brother started with his wife and family for Adelaide. He promised to write immediately on his arrival, and he kept his promise, though more than ten months elapsed before news of his safety came to his anxious friends. He had lost his wife and two of his three children during a tedious five month voyage.

Conditions on board these ships were often appalling. In 1835 as many as four adults slept in a berth six feet by four feet six inches, whereas convicts being transported had since 1790 been allowed four to a berth six feet square, in dormitories. Although in 1842 the Passengers Act prescribed for emigrants a minimum of nine square feet it was found as late as 1854 that 'few Emigrant Ships would have satisfied, the Admiralty specification for Convict Ships.'

Between 1787 and 1869 nearly 162,000 men and women were transported as convicts from Britain to her Australian colonies. 439 were sentenced for transportation by West Sussex Quarter Sessions between 1778 and 1853, and a further 53 were sentenced from other courts. Two convicts were from Walberton.

Thomas Ayling was committed on the 25 February 1821 to Petworth House of Correction. At the Easter Session at Petworth he was found guilty of stealing 11 capons worth 22/- and one hen worth 1/- the property of John Bristow of Washington. For this he was sentenced to seven years transportation, this seems excessive as usually transportation was given after a previous conviction.

William Cooper, labourer of Walberton was sent for trial at the General Quarter Sessions held at Horsham on 21st day of June 1831.

'With force and arms at the aforesaid Parish, stole on the 21st April, one copper furnace value of fifty shillings of the goods and chattel of Sir William Houston Knight (owner of Avisford House) then and there found feloniously did steal, take and carry away against the peace.'

He was found guilty of the offence and sentenced to be transported for 14 years.

Education

Horace Chalker, Schoolmaster at Walberton School 1874–1898, pictured with his wife, the Schoolmistress.

EDUCATION

In eighteenth century England there was no government organisation for education, but there was growing concern that some central provision should be made. Small groups of eminent men established Charity Schools, and occasionally, where there were benevolent gentry, Education Endowments were founded.

Walberton was fortunate in that the Lord of the Manor, John Nash, made provision in his will, dated 24th May 1732 for "A new built messuage, backside and garden in Walberton, and also an annuity of £12 to be used in the education and instruction of poor children of the said Parish for ever thereafter."

There was some sort of a school before this as the will mentions the Master, Charles Martin, as being allowed the use of the school and house "as long as he behaves well."

This school house was pulled down in about 1780, and another given for the use of the school. Later, due to lack of legal documents, this caused a dispute, for when General John White was the owner of Walberton house, the aid of Chancery had to be invoked in 1816 to compel him to allow the school to be used for its rightful purpose.

For those with financial means there has always been education, usually by private tutors or governesses, but for the majority there was no provision – so learning was gained from the family, Sunday Schools, or by whatever private means they could afford.

The idea that a national system of education should be established came from two sources. In 1808 the non-conformist Joseph Lancaster founded the British and Foreign School Society and the following year Andrew Bell began the National Society.

Lord Brougham's Commission in 1816 began to enquire into endowed charities and the Vicar of Walberton told the commissioners he was anxious that the National Society system of education (National Education in the Principles of the Established Church) should be introduced at Walberton. This came into effect when a grant of £30 was given for this purpose.

The 1841 census shows that the School Master was Raymond Ellis, aged 25 years, a married man with three children. He was also the enumerator for this census. Later, he moved to Barnham and became the Registrar of Births and Deaths for the area.

There survives a daily Register of Walberton National School which covers the period 25th November 1844 to 8th August 1845. There were 76 children registered at the beginning of this period, which increased to 113 by August. However, the actual average attendance was about 50. There was no schooling on Saturdays but the register kept for Sundays showed an attendance of 30 to 35.

Raymond Ellis, schoolmaster at Walberton in 1841.

A page from William Collins's copybook

WISDOM
excelleth
FOLLY
as far as
LIGHT
excelleth
DARKNESS

At the back of the Register, there are a few comments of interest:

November 1844: William Phillips – gone to the Union Home.
May 12th: False report on Monday by some of the children in telling others. Few present all week.
May 29th: Royal Oak Club Day. Holiday.
June 10th and 23rd: Took the children to church.
A footnote for weeks from Monday, June 16th to July 6th: 'Haying'.

Richard Prime, the owner of Walberton House, started to take an interest in the school in 1847 as described in the postscript of a letter to Richard Streatfeild

10th Oct 1847
Eliz. Vogan and Co. have got tired of the school and she writes to offer me the key to be given up tomorrow, and I shall appoint a Master and keep it henceforth without any subscribers or interference.

Richard Prime gave prizes to the children. A boy named William Collins was presented with a book which bore the inscription: *"Awarded to William Collins by Richard Prime Esq. for regular attendance and good behaviour during the year 1856 at Walberton School."*

At this time the school master was Thomes Elliot and the mistress Mrs Ann Randall. The high standard of copying can be seen from William Collins's copy book.

W.E. Forster's Education Act of 1870 required that there should be a sufficient number of schools for all children to attend. The school at Walberton was found to be inadequate for the number of children needing accommodation and the

Inspectors Report of 1872 recommended that a new school should be built. Arthur Prime of Walberton House undertook to build this school to house 80 boys and girls and 40 infants for the Walberton and Binsted School Districts. This scheme was delayed owing to the lack of alternative premises for carrying on schooling during the three months required for building the new school. Provision was eventually made in a barn belonging to Mr Prime, but ... "this cannot be warmed and the managers deem that it would not be suitable to transfer the children thither before the middle of March."

On the 2nd November 1874 the new school opened and on the first day twenty children registered, though the numbers gradually increased. Mr Horace Chalker was appointed as Master and remained at the school until 1898. He attended a training school in Norwich from 1850 to 1851 and became a certificated teacher while at St Mark's College, London in 1866. From the 1881 Census we know that he was aged 51 and that he and his wife Mary were born in Norwich. Their eldest son, William, 16 years, was a pupil teacher at Walberton School and their other five children were all scholars.

The school which was demolished in 1872.

This photograph of the new school, built on the same site as the old one, was taken after 1892 when Mr Ellis presented a bell, but the school funds were not sufficient to go to the expense of putting up a Bell-Cote so two concerts were given and the proceeds used for this purpose.

· BRENDA DIXON ·

The apparatus supplied for the school was: two easels; three blackboards; two maps; one dozen each standard Red Books, National Society and Graystone and Burkley's; sixteen dozen Darnell's copy books; three dozen slates; one box of chalks; twelve dozen pen holders; two gross pens; one gallon bottle of ink; two hundred slate pencils and one copy of Barnard Smith's *Arithmetic*.

The vicarage and others in the village sent books for the use of the Sunday and day school and also four pendent lamps for the use of the night school. Two forms and two chairs were given to the Sunday School.

Mr Chalker was helped by a pupil teacher and each week Mrs Vogan, the Vicar's wife, took a class for reading. The Vicar went to the school regularly as did Mrs Long and friends to inspect the sewing.

Below are some interesting entries from the School Log Book for the first year:

7th November 1874: Rousell family slack in their payments.

4th December 1874: Rousells went home as their school fees were in arrears. Nothing of note to record during the week, the usual school work gone through without the birching of a boy to break the monotony.

12th April 1875: Mrs Harden distributed some articles of underclothing to the older girls. The garments were made at

Mr Chalker with a class of boys in the late 1870s . . .

. . . and many years later with a class of girls.

the school and were given as rewards for attendance and cleanliness.

26th April 1875: Better attendance for each day of the week save Friday, when the children were in the woods and fields gathering flowers for "Garland Day" (May Day).

5th June 1875: The event of the week was a school feast-giving by Captain and Mrs Prime of Walberton House.

17th June 1875: On Thursday the Sunday School Children took tea at Mrs Hardens, Mill House.

19th July 1875: Several children made their appearance after the Registers were marked; the general excuse "Mothers' Wants".

1st November 1875: Received school clock.

Charles Ayling wrote an article for the *West Sussex Gazette* on the school feast held at Walberton House on the 5th June 1875.

A Brilliant School Treat

It is not the first time Mrs Prime has feasted our school children, and we are glad to say without distinction of sect, for Walberton of course must have its sects and religious divisions, as well as the great world around us. It was not only of an unusual proportion but it was held for the first time in the beautiful grounds of Walberton House The front of the mansion was decorated with festoons and flags - the signal bunting of Mr Prime's yacht - while other colours hung on poles in different parts of the grounds. About three o'clock the young ones marched from the school to the house, where under the colonnade, 183 sat down to tea, and such a tea as must have made many of them open their eyes as well as their mouths.

After the children had done their part, and done it well, they were sent off to play, while their mothers, sisters and friends took their places at the table.

The grounds were apparently open to all who chose to enter, and in the course of the evening the larger part of the villagers seem to have accepted the tacit invitation. Mr and Mrs Prime and others of the gentry, mingled freely with their unwonted visitors, evidently well pleased with the pleasures they had inspired.

The Vicar and Mrs Irvine were there and that gentleman in fact appeared to be director general of sports for the time, being in this well seconded by his two Lieutenants, Messrs, Maxwell (farm Bailiff) and Chalker. Judging by the applause that followed, two fire balloons sent up in the course of the evening gave most satisfaction.

Racing came next in favour because of the prizes, selected from a large table of toys in almost endless variety.

The following is part of a sonnet written by Charles Ayling about another school feast held in August 1879.

The stately mansions' noble colonnade,
Full charged with young humanity, with bright
And smiling faces beaming with delight,
In long extending, double ranks, arrayed,
Where novelty with plenty lies bestrewed,
And willing hands their every want supply,
Offers a pleasant picture to the eye
That loves the bright, the beautiful, the good.

When the *Walberton Almanack* was started by the Reverend Irvine in 1877, the following information was given about the school and the Elementary Education Act.

The School is maintained by Voluntary contributions, an Endowment of £12 a year, the Government Grant, and the School Fees.

The Managers are the Vicar of Walberton and the Rector of Binsted, Captain Prime (Walberton House), Sir W. Anson (Avisford House), Mr Clement (Secretary), Mr Upton and Mr Ellis, Mr Long, J.P. kindly acts as Treasurer – Mr R. Ellis as collector.

The total cost of maintaining the School last year was £113..14..1, of which £22..7.6, was produced by the Government Grant, and £3..16..3, by the school fees,

The Parish of Binsted contributes 1..6, of the expenditure."

Part of the Elementary Education Act for 1876 which concerned parents and labourers was reported in the *Almanack*.

Employers of labour will be liable to a fine of TWO POUNDS for allowing any child under nine years old to work for them or any child under eleven who has not got one of these certificates:

1. A certificate of having passed the second standard in a school under Government Inspection.

2. A certificate of having attended such a school for 250 times a year for two years.

NOTE – This law does not apply to children who live more than two miles from a school. Nor does it forbid the employment of children out of school hours, in the holidays and at special times (such as harvest) allowed by the School Committee of the District.

Parents will be liable to the same Fine of Two Pounds for employing their own children contrary to these regulations, or for giving a false certificate, or a false account of their children's age.

And a fine of FIVE SHILLINGS every fortnight for any child over five years of age who is found habitually idling about the streets or in bad company.

A further Act of 1880 raised the school leaving age to thirteen and tightened the regulations which allowed children to be absent. This obviously didn't have a great deal of effect in Walberton as there was continual concern over the number of children absent, which made the school Managers pass in April 1883 the following resolution.

The Managers will give a Bonus of 1..6 to every child who, haveing paid, the school fees and been present at the Government Inspector's Examination, shall have made 400 attendances in the school year ending May 31st, 1884; or a Bonus of 1s for 350 attendances.

On September 2nd, 1891 the Free Education Act came into operation and schools became entirely free. This caused the attendance at Walberton school to increase by about 20%.

That autumn the Sanitary Authority ordered the closing of the school for a month on account of the prevalence of scarlet fever. This was not the only time the school had to be closed due to infectious diseases and after one such closure in 1898 the Managers of the school were warned that the neglect by the caretaker was dangerous to the health and infringed the conditions of the grant.

> The closets and urinals are in a disgraceful dirty state ... the casks are full of filthy stagnant water. There is no supply of dry earth for the closets.

From the log book and the *Walberton Almanack* we can find out some of the subjects taught:

> Arithmetic, compound fractions, tables, money, mental arithmetic, addition and subtraction. Reading, recitation, pronounciation, grammer, spelling, dictation, composition and writing. Other subjects taught were sewing for girls, singing, history, geography and religious teaching.

In order to receive the government grant, National Society schools were examined once a year by the Diocesan inspector and Her Majesty's inspectors.

Religious teaching was of great importance and at the yearly Diocesan inspection the children were asked questions on the Old and New Testament and Catechism and the repetition of scriptures, hymns and Catechism were heard and they also had to write from memory. These examinations were always highly praised.

Her Majesty's Inspectors' reports were not always quite so satisfactory as remarks were made such as:

> "The children should not be allowed to count on their fingers."
> "The singing must improve or the grant lost."

The Inspector in 1886 was critical of the girls when they were weaker in all subjects, particularly in English and Spelling. Needlework was poor and nearly all the girls failed. For the same year, *"the infants could read, write and sum well, but they never have varied occupations."*

There was improvement the following year, but the inspector recommended that more attention be paid to the infants who he regarded as backward.

Charles Rowland became Schoolmaster on the 2nd January 1899 and his daughter Mary Jean was made Monitoress in the mixed room.

Charles Rowland, schoolmaster from Jan 1899.

The Rev Irvine still visited the school regularly as did his successor the Rev Crawley and also the Rev H.C.M Lewis of Binsted. The children attended Church Services on Ash Wednesday, Holy Thursday and five Saints days.

The following are a few entries from the Log Book for Mr Rowlands first year.

20th March 1899: Mrs Henty of Avisford House called and looked at the drawing; afterwards hearing the children sing.

23rd May 1899: The Wadeys have not attended as they have Typhoid Fever.

29th May 1899: Afternoon attendance lower than usual in consequence of annual club day being held in the Neighbourhood.

22nd June 1899: Sanitary Officer called. Misses Lewis, Smith and Raper called, in order to see the drill.

26th & 27th May 1899: The Whitty and Booker families absent on the account of measles.

30th June 1899: Attendance has fallen owing to measles.

20th July 1899: School not held this afternoon, the children being invited to a school treat at Mrs Henty's.

28th Sept. 1899: Miss Clark, Diocesan Lecturer gave an Elementary Science Lecture on alcohol.

23rd Oct. 1899: Mrs Crawley, the Vicar's wife, visited the school to distribute the prizes and certificates gained by scholars in an examination in connection with lecture given to the children on 28th Sept.

22nd Dec. 1899: Mrs Henty accompanied by Master and Miss Henty, distributed prizes to the children.

Mr Rowlands submitted to HM Inspector a scheme for teaching some class subjects. It is of interest that he suggested History for boys and Needlework for girls. Her Majesty's Inspector's report for his first year held on the 29th September showed that decided improvement had been made in discipline and attainments and the infants had made good progress.

The Diocesan Examination showed as usual all religious subjects to be either good or excellent.

Apart from the National School in Walberton there is evidence of four other small schools.

'Dame schools' as the name suggests were run by women in a room of their cottages, the better ones taught the children to read, write, perform simple sums, as well as teaching the girls to sew and knit.

One Dame school was taught by a Phebe Lucas who, according to the 1841 census was 75 years of age and a School Mistress. Her school was probably one of the better ones, as William Booker, one of its pupils, could write neatly, keep account books and became a successful businessman, butcher and farmer. Further information about him can be found in the section on Work and Play.

Another school was run by Miss Mary Cole White, 1809-94, who according to the same Census was a School Mistress and lived with her mother who had a grocers shop.

Over the door is printed: MARY COLE WHITE LICENSED DEALER IN TEA, COFFEE, TOBACCO.

This school was held in a back-room of the house and the residence is now called 'Roslyn'. By looking through the available directories we know that Mrs White, the mother, was a shopkeeper in 1832 and 1839. The next available directories are for 1852, 1855 and 1862, when Miss Mary Cole-White is recorded as a grocer. From the same source, we know that she was also Postmistress from 1867 to 1890.

Miss Mary Cole-White's premises, from which she ran a grocer's shop, post-office and 'dame school'.

Mrs Jean Dunn Ne Maxwell whose father was farm bailiff to Captain Prime of Walberton House, was born in December 1865 and was one of Miss Cole-White's pupils in the 1870's. Edward Humphrey, her brother-in-law, later wrote down her memories of the school.

"The entrance to the schoolroom was at the back of the house. There was when assembled, a room full of us boys and girls. We sat on long stools and occasionally the spirit of naughtiness would prompt a scholar to lift the stool from one side which left the unsuspecting remainder wriggling on the floor. The punishment inflicted on the guilty child when discovered was to be stood for a time on the door mat away from, but in view of, the class. On entering school we girls were obliged to curtsey and say 'Good morning Governess', while the boys made a salute. We learned by heart the collect for the day and also the catechism. The girls as a needlework lesson made samplers but I never became efficient in this. Miss White said I did not try. Miss White made a home for a cousin Edmund White and he was useful in running errands, working in the garden and orchard and other domestic jobs. It is said that Miss White in her kindness kept him from the workhouse. As well as her school Miss White kept a general shop and the village post office. Sometimes it was her nephew, Edmunds, duty to be in charge and he would occasionally put his head in at the schoolroom door and call 'shop'. Sometimes the schoolmistress would leave her teaching, closing the door behind her, and indulge in a lengthy gossip with a like-minded customer. When this happened the school was soon in hubbub; a veritable babel of voices. Then the Mistress's figure would appear in the doorway and the one commanding word 'silence' would fall from her lips. Soon the hubbub would begin again and so on till the interchange of news items between shopkeeper and customer was finished. Each week two girls were chosen to stay behind the rest and put the room tidy after school. The girls of which I was sometimes one, felt it something of an honour to be chosen for the task and feel a pride in viewing a tidy room from what had a few minutes before been a very untidy one. At Christmas time we went one morning specially for the 'breaking up'. There were no lessons that morning and after a short wait we all left the richer by the possession of an orange and a bun.'

Mary Cole-White   *Edward Cole-White*

In January 1935, G. Hotston of Littlehampton wrote to the *West Sussex Gazette* about his experiences at Miss Mary Cole White's School.

"I used to pay 3d per week for my schooling. There were also the Bookers (William, Charles, Allan), and I think, two sisters. There were also several of the Burches from the Holly Tree and the Hatchers from the Blacksmiths at the east end of the village. (Photos of these people taken many years later can be seen in the section on Work and Play.) The shop was at the south end of the house, the school in the centre and the north end was occupied by a gentleman they called 'old Edmunds'. When anyone came into the shop for coffee, our governess would give us a copper to go into the shop and grind some coffee for her; also for hunting snails in the box hedges around the flower borders. Any time during the afternoon, if she saw a cart or waggon come along going to Binsted, she would call to the carter to give us a ride home and hurry us up to get our clothing on , Binsted being rather far away and Walberton the nearest school."

A girls school was built in 1850 for Miss Packe, who was the daughter of Lady Elizabeth Reynell of Avisford House. Miss Leeming (who was also the church organist) was the school mistress. The reasons for starting such a school in a small village were probably twofold: to enable girls coming from a 'better class of family' such as those of the tradesmen to avoid mixing with the labourers' children, and to give Miss Packe, then aged 30, an occupation that would be regarded as respectable and worthwhile.

The school and house of Misses Packe and Leeming, The Street.

Miss Packe   *Miss Leeming*

Charles Ayling tells of this school in one of his articles:

Among other good works Mrs Paterson, while still Miss Packe, erected a neat block of buildings opposite the brewery as a school for village girls and a residence for the Mistress and this school she supported for several years until her marriage.

There is reference to this school in the *West Sussex Gazette* for 28th October 1869 when pupils of both Miss White's and Miss Leeming's schools joined with the National School for a treat. Nearly 200 children assembled for dinner 3.30pm and there was a large attendance of resident gentry to witness this pleasant scene. After the food, presents of clothing were given, followed by an exhibition of dissolving slides.

The fourth school in Walberton, run by Miss Farnden, was held at Myrtle Cottage. Miss Elizabeth Maxwell, later the wife of Edward Humphrey, attended this school.

At the time of the 1871 Census Miss Elizabeth Farnden, aged 27 years, ran a private school. Her mother, Eliza, a widow, lived with her as did her younger brother, Alfred, a solicitor's clerk.

In the latter half of the 19th century, Walberton had the benefit of two libraries, a reading and recreation room and courses of evening lectures. The *Almanack,* 1877 reports:

"There are now two lending libraries in the village – one at the vicarage, open every Saturday at twelve o'clock and another long established by Mrs Reynell Pack, at Avisford, open every Saturday at 11 o'clock."

·BRENDA DIXON·

Miss Elizabeth Farnden, Schoolmistress.

From Returns made by the Church Wardens in 1858 we know there was a library for the poor of the Parish.

In 1886, Sir William Jenner who was renting Avisford House gave 40 to 50 volumes to the lending library. An additional 60 volumes were given in 1893 by people living in Walberton and in 1898 some ladies of the parish put on 'an entertainment', raising £2..13..6 in aid of books for the Lending Library.

A Village Club and Reading Room was in 1883 started with a tea party and a request for books magazines, newspapers and games. By 1888 this institution had a good attendance and was open in the Vicarage Parish Room six nights a week throughout the season of six months. *The Almanack* for 1891 reports:

> "The Government is assisting liberally in establishing through-out the Country classes for Technical Education, as it is called ie. the teaching of useful trades and arts to those who have passed through our Parish Schools and others. At the present moment Laundry Work is being taught in the Vicarage by Miss Boader from Worthing. This will be followed by a course of classes on Cooking and Dairy Work; and for the lads, Drawing and Gardening (including fruit growing)."

In 1893 there were lectures and lessons on Horticulture when the average attendance was 17, but when a similar course was started in the autumn, it did not take and the cookery lessons were only thinly attended. Courses started at the beginning of the next year on "Nursing the Sick" followed by "Health in the Home" were more successful as were two further classes on "Sick Nursing".

Miss Farnden and pupils outside Myrtle Cottage.

· B R E N D A   D I X O N ·

Orthodox & Unorthodox Religion

Saint Mary's Church, Walberton.

ORTHODOX AND UNORTHODOX RELIGION

At the beginning of the 19th century there was in Walberton the established church of Saint Mary The Virgin; but by the end of the 1840's there were also two dissenting Chapels.

The Reverend Thomas Vogan, who was appointed Vicar of Walberton in 1843, was 'high church' and his views were not liked by some parishioners. Evidence for this can be found in a letter from Mrs Prime to Richard Streatfeild.

4th November 1845

[The Reverend Vogan] . . . our beast, savage beast has now put the finishing stroke to the devotion in our Parish; the people say he is bad in the pulpit, and still worse out of it; — so yesterday a person came to see either Mr Prime or myself (I was at home) to ask if Mr Prime would sell a piece of ground for the erection of a place of Worship; of course I said no but the person vividly said,

"we must be able to go to a place of worship and we will not go to Vogan's Church. Mr Paul from Worthing is very rich and he will build and buy a bit of land from someone in the parish for the purpose!"

Can the Bishop sleep in quiet in his bed and think of the mischief he has done?

Mr Paul of Worthing belonged to a sect known as the Bible Christians which was founded in 1815 by W. O. Bryan a Wesleyan preacher.

The start of this church is described in notes from the dairy of William Atkin, reader to the Mission at Worthing. These were read out at a meeting held in November 1897 to celebrate the 50th Anniversary of this Chapel.

Sep 30th 1845. Went to Walberton for the first time with Mr Paul, found a few friends assembled at Mr Ayling's, about 13 small and great, promised to see them once a fortnight. (This Mr Ayling lived at Jasmine Cottage and is not the Charles Ayling who wrote the articles and poems.)

Jan 6th 1846. A very wet morning, went to Walberton and held the meeting, about 22 present.

Feb 3rd 1846. Went to Walberton with Mr Paul. Formed the little church, about 22 communicants, several spoke their experience and shed many tears.

Feb 17th 1846. Went to Walberton. In a crowded room the first child from Westergate was Baptized.

Nov 25th 1846. Went with Mr Paul to Walberton to the communion. Mr Ayling presented a piece of ground for a small new chapel. Although the rain was falling heavily about 45 assembled for tea and a very happy evening was spent.

Nov 30th 1847. The little Chapel was publicly opened. A tea meeting was held, folowed by a religious service when addresses were given by William Atkins and other Christian Ministers and friends.

The strength of the church grew and by 1886 the new Baptist Chapel was completed. Charles Ayling wrote about,

OUR NEW CHAPEL [*The old Chapel was retained for the use of the Sunday School, but is now a garage opposite the paper shop.*]

The dissenting half of the village held high festival yesterday week, the occasion being the opening of their new chapel, an event naturally of much interest and importance to our little community. Friends came in large numbers from Worthing, Angmering, Arundel and elsewhere. The first part of the programme was a religious service in the Chapel and this was presently followed by a large tea party in Mr Humphrey's meadow . These alfresco tea drinkings are very pleasant and jolly affairs. In the evening, there was a crowded, or rather an overcrowded, public meeting. This meeting had one result which does not always attend such gatherings. An appeal being made for assistance in defraying the cost of the building and the ground, the response was so hearty and so effective, that the whole sum required was subscribed or promised on the spot. That was a very satisfactory result and we congratulate our nonconformist friends on being able to start on their new career with no debt hanging about their necks. The chapel is about twice the size of the one it supersedes which is to be retained as a schoolroom. It was built by Mr Sergant, of Walberton, from designs by Mr Moore, a Worthing architect.

From the Minute Book for March 1900.

During the summer of 1899 some of the Brethren and sisters wished to confess their faith in Christ by Baptism;(Total Im-

The new Baptist Chapel, 1886.

· BRENDA DIXON ·

mersion of Adults) it was suggested that a Baptistry should be made in the chapel, a fund was started and with united help £18..8..9 raised. Mr William Sergant executed the work and put the pipe from the pump in the Chapel into his own well in the Malthouse allowing us the use of it when wanted for which a payment is to be made of one shilling a year.

March 7th 1900. The Baptistry was used for the first time, the meeting commenced by singing and prayers. While the opening Hymn was being sung one of our Sisters came in and not knowing where the Baptistry was made fell into the pool, this caused a little consternation, she was quickly lifted into the vestry and went home at once, none the worse for the accident except being frightened.

The Wesleyan Methodists meeting place as such no longer exists. Their services were held at the invitation of the Miller, Solomon Short, in what used to be part of the grain store in Mill Lane.

There are short references to this meeting house in some of Charles Ayling's articles where he mentions temperance tea parties' being held. The *West Sussex Gazette* occasionally reported Missionary Society meetings such as, The Annual Missionary Society meeting held on December 2nd, 1869 which was well attended and £6..4..2 raised

Walberton came under the Chichester District Methodist Circuit and from the Baptism Records kept from 1840 it is known that Solomon, son of Solomon and Mary Short was Baptized on January 10th 1849. This is the first record mentioning Baptism from Walberton and the last entry from the Village was in 1912.

The Religious Census of 1851 which was filled in by Solomon Short, Chapel Leader and Miller gave the numbers attending the service held in the afternoon as twenty-five.

Mr Hartley and Mr Short represented Walberton at the Circuit Quarterly Meetings and in December 1894 reference was made to the death of Mr Ewens, a local Preacher, who had been a devoted member of Walberton Church since 1856. In March 1901 the question of a new Chapel was discussed and Mr Short suggested that the next meeting should be held at Walberton where there would be a hearty welcome and tea. At this meeting the question of the chapel was raised again and by the September £10 had been placed in the bank. This Chapel was never built and Walberton Methodists transferred to Barnham or Westergate in the early 1900s.

Many Sunday School treats were reported in the *West Sussex Gazette*. Here are just two from Walberton: one nonconformist and one Church of England.

The unorthodox half of young Walberton must have looked a little bit glum on Wednesday, last week. It was the day appointed for the annual feast of the dissenting Sunday Schools and the weather, from a holiday point of view was perfectly shameful, more adapted for growing turnips than alfresco feasting. The affair was to have come off as usual in Mr Humphrey's meadow, but because of the rain, a large house standing empty and idle close at hand was compelled to make itself useful for the occasion and under its ample shelter a large and happy party sat down to the indispensable tea. The weather brightened up towards evening and permitted the little ones to finish off the day with some open air games."

"This week we have to record the festive doings of our Church going juveniles, with the members of the Church choir, who held high festival in the grounds of the vicarage a few days ago. This party had the advantage of a fine day and very sensibly made the most of it. The older girls played stoolball — a feminine form of cricket — younger ones were racing and so were the boys. A still younger group had a 'scramble' for gingerbread and sweets which the Lady of the vicarage scattered with a liberal hand."

St Marys Church, although in the centre of the village, is in a secluded situation off The Street, surrounded by tall trees. Charles Ayling's articles and poems give a delightful feeling for this ancient church and churchyard.

When strangers from a distance spend a few hours in a country village, few of them fail to devote a few minutes to the church and churchyard. With summer visitors to Walberton it is a frequent subject of remark, almost of complaint, that they cannot find the church. From its position and specially when the trees are wreathed in summer robes, it is not easy to catch sight of it while passing through The Street. and yet it is not far away and he will find it a very pleasant spot. Few country graveyards are better situated for those who enjoy a

few minutes 'meditation among the tombs'. Shut out from the village and almost surrounded by shrubberies, which only half conceal the handsome pleasure grounds of an adjoining seat, a visitor may, if so disposed, resign himself to hours of solitude and reflections, if inclined first to take a view of the outer world, a glance westward will show a pleasant, if not very diversified landscape, the Chichester Cathedral spire standing out as the most prominent feature, while the Isle of Wight, like a misty cloud, may generally be seen in the background far away. The spot is kept in neat order, probably at the Vicar's expense, but the shrubs have grown too luxuriantly and might with advantage be replaced by smaller specimens. Of the church itself, its exterior cannot be called handsome, but aesthetically, it is to our eyes exceedingly beautiful.

Robert Hardy was Vicar at Walberton from 1801 to 1843; in the Vestry Minute Book for this period can be found the amount paid in land tax for the upkeep of the church. Among the usual entries for bills paid for such items as cleaning the church, washing the surplice and wine for sacrament, there was up until Easter 1815, money paid out for sparrow heads and hedgehogs. In 1806, three shillings and four pence was paid for 20 dozen sparrow heads, and for 12 dozen hedgehogs, two shillings and fourpence. According to an old Sussex farming belief, hedgehogs spoiled the cows' milk by sucking their teats while they lay asleep in the fields.

The wall round the churchyard was in a very dilapidated state and Richard Prime of Walberton House offered, in 1834, to repair the existing wall on the East side if Parishioners would

· U N K N O W N   T O   H I S T O R Y   A N D   F A M E ·

build a new wall round the rest of the churchyard. In the same year he offered at his own expense 'to render the church more dry' and to improve the churchyard by having the grass mown rather than allowing in sheep or other cattle which constantly damaged the tombstones.

Whilst the soil from against the church was being removed and an underground drain constructed, an ancient stone coffin, probably of Saxon origin, was discovered lying across the porch door. This can now be seen in the church.

In 1842 several improvements were carried out. The Vestry agreed that Mr Yorke's estimate of £8 for a pulpit, reading desk and Communion Table should be accepted and that Mr Caiger be paid £2..50 for whitewashing the church. Also that year we find that: 'Complaints have often been made that boys are often noisy during Divine Service and in the churchyard, before and after, it is hereby resolved to appoint Joseph Cole as Beadle with orders to punish such as offend and if he held such office for a year to pay him half a sovereign at the end of it.''

The Reverend Dr Thomas Vogan was Vicar of Walberton from 1843 to 1875. By the time of the 1851 Census he was fifty years old and lived with his wife Mary in the Vicarage. They employed three unmarried house servants. Mrs Vogan supported and conducted a Sunday School, and ran a general clothing club.

The Rev Thomas Vogan, Vicar of Walberton and Yapton, 1843-1875.

This descriptive poem on memories of the church and churchyard was published in the *West Sussex Gazette* on May 22nd 1862.

One spot, a sacred spot within our village pale.
Can tempt my wandering feet, can prompt my unpretending tale;
Too seldom sought, I seek it now, delighted to behold
Its shingled spire, with lettered vane, surmounted as of old.

Who does not love the village church that tells of other times?
Who can forget the music of its far resounding chimes?
Who does not sigh at thought of some that slumber in its shade?
What happy bosom does not know the vacuum death has made?

Its tall and not ungraceful spire points heavenward still and time
Has lightly touched it in his flight, restless and sublime;
But much within its massive walls of novelty is found,
For time and taste and gold have thrown a wondrous change around.

The galleries are gone, the pews displaced, the pulpit scarce the same,
Nor that the font where I received my brief baptismal name.
Half vexed to see and yet compelled, in candour to admire,
Scarce wakening sadness — still the change leaves something to desire.

In this poem Charles Ayling mentioned the old font and gallery and from the vestry minutes it is possible to discover when these changes occurred.

Apparently in 1843 the Archdeacon of the Diocese objected to the font and so it was authorized by the church wardens to provide a better one for a 'trifling sum' — that font having been used for 'time out of mind'.

A meeting of the vestry was called in 1857 for the purpose of determining on the removal of the remainder of the gallery and at this meeting it was agreed it should be taken down.

According to Charles Ayling, a slightly incongruous assortment of individuals used to assemble up a loft in the large gallery.

They did their best, there was a bass viol almost as big as the performer, a flute, two clarinets and another instrument which we youngsters irreverently called a horses leg — perhaps it was an oboe.

The ancient font, removed from St Mary's in 1843.

St Mary's church interior, prior to alterations in 1903.

The churchyard contains a few interesting grave stones which Charles Ayling referred to in an article dated June, 1864.

A walk round a country churchyard not only offers material for reflection but will sometimes provoke a smile even in our most serious moments by the quaint and curious epitaphs and inscriptions not unfrequently found. Our village graveyard contains three stones of a somewhat remarkable aspect — not so much for the letter press, if we may so call it, as for the engravings — pictures in stone which tell in no mistakable language the fate of those that sleep below.

The first represents the death of a child, killed by a cask, apparently a butter tub, falling from the tail of a cart, the shafts having escaped from the hands of an affrighted urchin, who is standing horror struck at the catastrophe of which he appears to have been the involuntary cause.

The second picture shows the doom of one who was drowned at sea, so the inscription tells us. Village tradition adds that it was a smuggler who lost his life in pursuing his perilous, but at the time very popular, avocation. The sculpture seems to justify the opinion. A revenue cutter in full sail occupies the centre of the stone. An individual of somewhat magnified proportions, being nearly half as tall as the cutters mast, is leaning over her side watching a sea fight of a very novel character which is taking place on the water below. The cutters boat is engaging the smugglers craft, which evidently has the worst of it, four of the crew being seen struggling in the sea, two of them directly under the boat which the victorious enemy (having seized it by the bows) are pushing stern foremost under the water, a mode of deciding a naval action which Nelson possibly never thought of.

· B R E N D A   D I X O N ·

The third stone is of more ambitious pretensions. Being near a hundred years old (now 200 years) it was a while ago completely obscured by a coat of luxuriant, lichen but has been recently restored in very creditable style — we believe by Mr Booker our village artist in stone. The original sculptor of this affair was not destitute of talent; his work will bear inspection even now and is of a very elaborate character. The inscription which tells us that he lost his life by the fall of a tree, is decidedly superfluous, for there is the tree itself, its cumbrous arms crushing out his life. A fellow workman with an axe in one hand, lifts the other in affright. Old Time with scythe and hour glass and a well developed fore lock, is also there, while the grim and grinning skeleton, the lord of all that lives, stands about to plunge an arrow into the helpless sufferer. At the top of the stone a figure with a glory round its head holds the sacred volume open at a very apposite passage, "Where the tree falls there it shall be", and on either side a full-blown cherub sounds the judgement summons, while each upper corner of the stone is formed of an inverted cornucopia, pouring its treasures on the group below.

The Reverend William Irvine became Vicar of Walberton in 1875. Two years later he was the originator of the *Walberton Almanack and Parish Register* which continued until 1898. He lived in the Vicarage with his wife and six children and from the 1881 census it is known that the eldest sons were twelve years old and probably twins and the youngest five. Another boy of 8 years lived with them as a pupil. All of the children were taught by a governess. Other living-in servants were a cook, housemaid and nursemaid.

These illustrative headstones from Walberton churchyard tell the stories of —

a child killed by a falling cask . . .

. . .a man drowned at sea . . .

. . . and another killed by a falling tree.

The Rev William Irvine, Vicar of Walberton from 1876-1899.

The Rev William Crawley was Vicar of St Mary's from 1899. While the incumbent, he invited the Church Army to hold a Mission on the Green. Pictured below is Captain Boyce with some of the village boys. He was a Church Army Captain in the early 1900s and in charge of the Chichester No.1 Van for 1902-4. He worked in the Archdeaconry of Chichester and during 1903 sold Bibles and books and held 21 missions.

The Rev William Crawley, who became Vicar in 1899, pictured with his family.

· BRENDA DIXON ·

SMUGGLING AND THE CHURCH

In the past Walberton church and churchyard had been involved with smugglers, and the Reverent Robert Hardy was very concerned with this problem and in 1818 published a pamphlet on this subject. Below is the front page and an extract from this pamphlet.

SERIOUS

CAUTIONS AND ADVICE

To all concerned in

S M U G G L I N G ;

SETTING FORTH

The Mischiefs attendant upon that Traffic:

TOGETHER WITH SOME

EXHORTATIONS TO PATIENCE & CONTENTMENT

UNDER THE

Difficulties and Trials of Life.

By ROBERT HARDY, A. M.

VICAR OF THE UNITED PARISHES OF WALBERTON AND YAPTON, AND OF STOUGHTON IN SUSSEX; AND CHAPLAIN TO H. R. H. THE PRINCE REGENT.

" Whatsoever is brought upon thee, take cheerfully, and be patient when thou art changed to a low estate. For gold is tried in the fire, and acceptable men in the furnace of adversity. Believe in Him and He will help thee : ORDER THY WAY ARIGHT, and trust in Him."

Ecclus. ii. 4—6.

London:

PRINTED FOR F. C. AND J. RIVINGTON, 62, ST. PAUL'S CHURCH-YARD ;

By M. Mason, East Street, Chichester.

1818.

* Smuggling has not been confined to the lower orders of people ; but, from what I have heard, I apprehend, that it has been very generally encouraged by their superiors, for whom no manner of excuse, that I know of, can be offered. I was once asked by an Inhabitant of a Village near the sea, Whether I thought there was any harm in Smuggling? upon my replying, that I not only thought there was *great deal of harm* in it, but *a great deal of sin ;* he exclaimed, " Then the Lord have mercy upon the County of Sussex, for who is there that has not had a tub !" *The harm* of the Trade—to the poor, imprisoned labourer especially—if not *the sin* of it, is now made sufficiently apparent : and I hope there are many in " the County of Sussex," who will have nothing to do with " a Tub" in future.

Charles Ayling writes on his childhood memories of smuggling tales and times.

On the south side of our parish church there may still be seen several large heavy looking tombs built of brick and covered with large flat stones and old smugglers have often told us that the interior of the tombs were favourite places of temporary deposit for contraband articles. We have also heard it from the lips of the parish clerk himself, an old fellow of nearly 90 years — that he had known goods hidden in the church itself. The pulpit, now demolished, was a large, hollow, old fashioned affair and we have seen our selves moveable panels near the bottom by which the "tubs" were introduced, while silks and light portable articles were deposited in the sounding-board overhead. In the early part of the century half of Walberton seem to have been smugglers and not by any means the poorer half. One of our large farmers, who died within the memory of most of us, was not only a smuggler. but a sort of captain over them. Smuggling, like poaching, was not considered a crime; those only were criminals who had the bad luck to be caught. It must have been in 1828 or 29 a brother called to us to see a troop of men coming over the Green, each carrying two or three barrels strung over their shoulder. One was a next door neighbour and the goods were to be left at his house, but that same afternoon we saw those same tubs hastily thrown over his garden wall and deposited in a ditch at the back of our own. Officers entered the house to search it just ten minutes too late. One nutting season we went up to Pot Hill Copse at the back of the house and there we found some of the farmer's tubs, hid in the brushwood for the day. We "requisitioned" one of the tubs, and took it home and my sisters handed it round, until a regular jollification was the result.

The Yew tree in Walberton chuchyard.

Pubs, Brewing
& Teetotallers

PUBS, BREWING AND TEETOTALLERS

Alcoholic consumption in Britain reached a peak in 1875/6. Beer drinking had greatly increased since 1830 when an Act was passed enabling virtually any householder, for a small fee, to sell beer on the premises. This Act had been passed in the hope that the amount of gin drunk would decrease by encouraging beer consumption. Drinking only started to be considered as a problem with the realisation that excessive alcohol consumption affected standards of work and added to the problems of the low-paid and unemployed. This was difficult to resolve, as drink was cheap and traditionally part of everyday life and custom.

There are three pubs within Walberton's village boundaries and Charles Ayling describes their signs.

The signs of our village pubs have something poetical about them. The insignia of one house suggests oak apples and loyalty (The Royal Oak), another holly berries (The Holly Tree), and a merry Christmas; while in our juvenile days the third house was often referred to under the pleasant euphemism of the 'Beggar's Opera' (The Balls Hut, now The Fontwell). Will any one venture to say that a village like this, with only 607 separate throats, including teetotallers, old maids, children, parsons, penniless people, and babes at breast can possibly require three public houses to supply it with drink? Yet here they are, all three of them, and all as we suppose doing a living, if not a lively business, unless they are simply starving each other; while just beyond the village boundary, lying well within sight of it, and none of them more than half a mile distance there are six other open houses, already to give you a warm and hearty welcome if only you are willing and able to pay for it. So put money in your purse, you need not go far to get drunk!.

Publicans of 'The Holly Tree' The Street, Walberton 1867–90	
1867	George Burch
1881	Matthew Cob
1885	Alan Bowley
1889	Egbert Townley
1889	James Cooper
1890	William Johnson

George Burch worked as a carrier and beer retailer in 1852 and then in 1867 he applied for a licence for the Holly Tree Inn and continued there as publican until 1881. While he was the proprietor the Inn was sold by auction on Monday July 26th 1875, being purchased by the Eagle Breweries Arundel.

*Barmaids stand outside
The Holly Tree Inn.*

*The same pub some years later
after considerable refurbishment.*

Alan Bowley, put this advertisement in W.T. Pikes *District Blue Book*, 1886. He left the Holly Tree Inn in 1888 but continued his work as a carrier, coal merchant and fly proprietor in the village.

HOLLY TREE INN,
WALBERTON,
NEAR ARUNDEL,
One and a half miles from Barnham Junction Station.

....

CHOICE WINES & SPIRITS,
ALES AND STOUT.

....

Every Accommodation for Families and Visitors.
PRIVATE APARTMENTS.

BROUGHAM OR WAGGONETTE ON HIRE.
Any Train met b appointment, either at Arundel (3½ miles)
or Barnham Junction.

....

Good Stabling and Coach-houses.

....

WOOD, COAL, AND COKE MERCHANT.

....

Carrier to Chichester Wednesdays and Saturdays.

....

ALLAN BOWLEY, Proprietor.

Among Charles Ayling's articles is this unusual one on a baby show at the Inn.

The novelty of a baby show made some slight noise in the village last week and offered pleasant proof that we are able to raise a crop of babies in spite of bad seasons and hard times. The exhibition came off at the Holly Tree, but the presiding genius of the affair seems to have been a Mr Cheap John, or "Cheape Jack" — we are not sure of the correct appellative — who spent the week in bleeding our village pocket, and who possibly got up this infantine cattle show as an additional means of inducing the current coin to flow freely. For the credit of our Walberton west end we are happy to say the prize — for good looks, and condition — was awarded to our little next door neighbour, Master Edward Sydney Burch, aged at half a year or thereabouts. From personal observation we can attest he has a pair of beautiful blue eyes — his mothers gift — and unless our ears now and then deceive us, he has also a pair of very sound lungs — his father's gift. The little fellow treats the distinction with perfect indifference and considers the prize of a copper kettle beneath his notice.

When Charles Ayling was a child his brother took him to the Ball's Hut Inn to see a Badger Baiting.

A PASTIME OF THE PAST
We can just remember when our big brother, in our very juvenile days, took us to the Ball's Hut to see a badger baiting — the last we ever heard of in the village. On reaching the spot he deposited his little charge on the top of a wall — out of

harms way. It made a strong impression on a small child, the more vividly, perhaps, as it was the only badger we saw and the only time we ever saw a badger — that is a living specimen. How we trembled at the thought of the terrible animal in that mysterious tub. When the dogs first entered the tub there was a terrible set to, and one half — drunken idiot, whose dog was getting the worst of it, put his arm into the tub to pull it out, and when he withdrew his hand, which he did very quickly, we caught our first view of the badger. The poor little brute had fastened its teeth through the palm of the big brute's hand, and held it fast. How the fellow bellowed and blubbered, and roared, till his comrades, by tugging and cuffing, and half choking compelled the animal to release the hand and retreat into its den. It had a brief respite while the man's

paw was balsamed and bandaged and then the 'fun' began again. The badger, making a bold leap for life, came out of its fortress, dashed through the crowd around, and before anyone could well understand what it was about, it was over the fence and fairly on its way to Slindon Wood, With a roar of rage and disappointment, the whole bevy of brutes on two legs set off after the runaway. Our big brother was among them, and left alone, terrified and trembling, we scrambled from the wall, and ran away also. Twenty years after we saw the mark of the badger's teeth on the man's hand, and heard him tell with a grin how many times he got drunk, without expense, over that lucky bite.

The *West Sussex Gazette* in 1861 describes a lively function that took place at the Royal Oak Inn.

· BRENDA DIXON ·

The annual ball at the Royal Oak Inn took place on Monday 31st December, when a nice party assembled fully bent on dancing the old year out and the new one in; and to enliven the scene twelve non-commissioned officers of the Royal Marine Artillery made their appearance from Fort Cumberland, During their stay their liberality to strangers and the manner in which they conducted themselves throughout is deserving of great credit. The next day after partaking of an excellent dinner, provided by Mrs Todman, They left the house in an orderly manner and proceeded to the Yapton Station.

Apart from these three pubs, Lucy Cooper, a widow, was licensed for the drinking of beer on her premises from 1869 to 1872. In September 1871 she met with a serious accident which was reported in the *West Sussex Gazette*.

A poor woman named Lucy Cooper who keeps a beer house was going to Arundel about her license when she was thrown out of her cart when her pony stumbled.

The Royal Oak Inn

M. ELLIS & SON,

PALE ALE & STOUT BREWERS

And Maltsters,

THE BREWERY, WALBERTON.

NEAR ARUNDEL.

LIST OF PRICES.

Qualities.				Kild.	Firkins.	Pins.
XXXX Strong Ale	...	...	...	30/-	15/-	7/6
XXX Mild	...	...	...	27/-	13/6	6/9
XX Mild	...	..	...	18/-	9/-	4/6
Pale Ale	...	...	...	18/-	9/-	4/6
Double Stout	...	...	...	27/-	13/6	6/9
Porter	..	...	..	18/-	9/-.	4/6

Allsopp & Co.'s Ales and Guinness's Stout, in Cask or Bottle.

BOTTLED ALES AND STOUT.

MALT AND HOPS SUPPLIED.

Telegrams and Goods to Barnham Junction, London, Brighton, and South-Coast Railway.

There were several small maltsters in the village during the nineteenth century, and the following are the names of brewers and maltsters taken from the Trade Directories.

1832 Ellis & Farnden. Further entry in 1839
1852 Edward Ellis. Further entries in 1858, 1862 and 1867.
1874 Mrs Matilda Ellis, brewer & maltster. Further entry, 1878
1887 Mrs Matilda Ellis & Son, brewer & maltster. Further entries in 1890, 1899 and 1903.
1890 Fredrick Thomas Levett, manager to the above.
1903 George W. Tanner, also manager to the above.

The main maltsters and brewers premises can still be seen and are situated on The Street, close to the Yapton Lane Junction.

Brewing would have been carried out in the village many years before the recorded entry in the Rates Book of 1800 when Ellis and Farnden were paying rates for the Brew house. By 1813 the name Farnden was dropped from these rates, though he paid separately for the Malthouse. This Brewery remained in the Ellis family until it closed in the 1920s.

The price list of Ellis's brewery, 1886.

Walberton Brewery

TEETOTALLERS

Concern over the volume of alcoholic intake gave rise to the temperance movement, and two such organizations were trying to encourage members in Walberton. One was run by the Established Church and the other by the Non-conformists.

From the *Walberton Almanack* we find that a branch of the Church of England's Temperance Society started in 1882. It began with a public meeting, held in the schoolroom, on March 25th, when an address was given setting forth the objects of the society. Monthly meetings were held in the Vicarage Parish Room, and the number of members gradually increased to thirty nine, twenty one belonging to the Temperance Section, ten to the Total Abstaining and eight to the Juvenile. The secretary for the society was Mark Luxford, the miller.

Charles Ayling writes about how the Vicar took this group to the 'Health Exhibition':

The village sent a very respectable contingent to the 'Healtheries' last week. The members consisting chiefly of the Church Temperance Society, must have seen a good many things to wonder at and admire.

Good Templars

Walberton is moving on. We have a branch of the Order of Good Templars established in the village. Our village Templars have begun business in a business-like manner. They have opened a Temperance Hall, and we intend presently to step in, and, over a cup of coffee, discuss temperance subjects with their leading spirits. At the last meeting a resolution was proposed, and carried which must have made a certain Mr Ellis of Walberton Breweries turn pale down to the very tips of his toes. So soon as they are strong enough to carry the resolution into effect, the brewery is to be converted into baths and wash-houses — a very useful reform, but possibly not an easy one, So far as their aims are sensible, useful, and practical we wish them success. They are engaged in a good cause, the human soul is worth a struggle, even when tottering, defaced and well-nigh ruined by the demon drink. Money, like drink, does much mischief in the world, but who will say that it does no good? The world for a good many years to come will have to find room both for the public house and the liquor trade as they are deeply-rooted English institutions and our temperance friends have a tough task before them if they intend to destroy it root and branch. It is the 'Fifth Estate' of the realm. Queen, Lords, Commons, and newspapers at present claim a right of precedence, but for how long in the teeth of trade unions and universal suffrage is a point for the future to decide. Speaking locally, but with an eye to the tendency of the age, we have sad misgivings that our dear old village church will be 'disestablished' long before either the 'Holly Tree' or the 'Oak'.

Our excellent friends the Good Templars were holding high festival at the Wesleyan Chapel over cake and tea. 'The cup that cheers but not inebriates' seemed to have a very cheering effect, for the mingling voices rose and fell in lusty, but very pleasant song.

Work & Play

WORK & PLAY

Villages in the 19th century still produced many of the goods and services required to support the community. This pattern gradually changed with the advance of industrial society and in particular with improved communications, better roads and transport, which brought the railway to the area in 1846; the Bognor via Barnham to London line opened in 1864.

Walberton did not have its own Doctor, but relied on John Boniface Collins, who came from Yapton, and whose sons carried on the practice after him. He was admitted as a member of the Royal College of Surgeons on 19th April 1860. Charles Ayling wrote the following in praise of him.

> "The village on the whole, must be a healthy one; neither epidemics nor endemics, nor zymotics, or any other 'ics' find a place among us; or if they come, they are quickly stamped out. this reflects credit on the care and skill of our excellent local practitioner Dr Collins, though we are sorry to hear he does not himself enjoy the best of health. If we were 'called in' to prescribe for him we should recommend him to leave Yapton and try our Walberton air."

The vaccination acts of 1861 and 1871 required every child to be vaccinated for smallpox before it was three months old, or at the next public vaccination held in the district after the child had attained that age. This was carried out at the Shoulder of Mutton Inn, Yapton and at the Newburgh Arms, Slindon.

Many villagers could not afford to see the doctor for ordinary ailments and 'cures' were passed on through families and friends. Henry Pesket, who was the village postman in the 1880s, copied out such a recipe: a cure for the 'hooping cough'.

Dr John Boniface Collins

"Take one quart of good beer, not very new. Put into it a good handful of common thyme, and boil it till it is reduced to a pint, then strain it and sweeten it with sugar candy. When the cough is coming on, if an infant give it a tea spoonful, and for a large child a table spoonful."

In 1871, Henry Peskett was 26, married and had one son. Ten years later he had six children and his mother-in-law lived with them. His occupation was "bootmaker and letter carrier". When, in 1894, Miss White retired from her duties at the Post Office, he became Postmaster and took over the telegraph station, which had been established in the village in 1890.

Pictured below is the 'Telegraph Office' and part of the cottage where Henry Peskett and his family lived.

Henry Peskett, village Postmaster, pictured outside John Humphrey's shop in The Street.

· BRENDA DIXON ·

John Humphrey, who was born in Littlehampton, came to work in Walberton in 1856 for Messrs Henwood and Stonham in their drapery and grocery business. He kept an account book which gives details of his salary and progress in those early years until he started his own shop in 1861.

1856, March 28 – Engaged with Mefs^n Henwood & Stonham, Walberton Sussex in the Drapery & Grocery Business for £15-0-0 Per Annum.

1857, April 15 – Mefs^n Henward and Stonham gave up their Business at Walberton to Moses and Alfred Moase. Engaged with them for £15-0-0.

1859, July 15 – Raised my Salary to £20-0-0

January 1 – Raised my Salary to £24-0-0

Sept 1 Raised my Salary to £25-0-0

Oct 14 Left Walberton and Engaged to Alfred Moase, Pulboro' Sussex for the same Money.

1860, June 9 – Left Alfred Moase and Engaged with Mefs^n Hide & Everett, Walberton Sussex for £30-0-0 Per Annum. Left March 1st 1861.

In 1862 he married Ann Farnden, the daughter of a maltster. The photograph opposite shows an embroidery sampler she worked at the age of nine.

They had five children — three girls and two boys; Henry and Edward (Edward took many of the photographs in this book) and both helped with the family business. Tragically, the two eldest daughters, Alice and Ada, died of a fever after drinking water from an infected well.

Alice Humphrey

Ada Humphrey

The third daughter, Mary married the son of the farm bailiff, John Maxwell, and Edward married Maxwell's daughter. The following is part of a letter Mary wrote to Elizabeth Maxwell.

Walberton, December 1st 1891

My Dear Liz,

There is such a lot to do before Xmas. Miss Irving invited me to help in a concert, also Carie, Bess and the rest. Of course we all declined. Last year we were invited to a servants ball at Avisford, my nose felt like elevating itself several inches in the air.

Yesterday father had a note from Mrs Irving saying that they wanted to have a tea and Christmas Tree for <u>all</u> the children of the day school,* would he as a manager like to help; I answered it for him and offered my assistance towards furnishing the tree so shall have to bustle round. She came down to thank me for my letter.

Then there is a series of lessons to be held in the parish room under Lady Anson's patronage for cooking, washing etc. I do not know if it will be a success or not.

We are going to have the fortnightly service of the Wesleyans in our chapel tonight as their place is being put in repair. We are going to have a prayer meeting at Carries tonight before the service (ladies only). I have never been to one of the kind so feel interested. We had very good congregations on Sunday both morning and evening. We had twenty four at the prayer meeting last night, very good, wasn't it?

---

* From the School Log Book: "The Managers and some Lady friends, gave the school children a tea and Christmas Tree. The presents were many, good and useful."

WALBERTON, *18 Apr* 189*8*

Mr A Booker

Bought of J. HUMPHREY,
DRAPER, GROCER, TEA DEALER,
PROVISION MERCHANT AND BUTCHER.

BISCUITS OF ALL KINDS.

China, Glass, Earthenware & Ironmongery.
Boots and Shoes.
P A T E N T   M E D I C I N E S.

HUMPHREY, GROCER & DRAPER.

The Humphrey's business flourished and grew from the single premises to incorporate three separate units for the drapery, grocers and butchers, by the end of the century.

There were other shopkeepers in the village and the photograph below shows the grocers shop in The Street which was run by James Johnson Bell and his daughter Louisa, who was 26 years old in 1881. She owned a 'brougham' which could be hired to take passengers to Barnham station.

Another shopkeeper mentioned in the Local Directory for 1866–7 was Samuel Shipton. Four years later, according to the 1871 census, he was 47 years old and his occupation was that of general carrier. The photograph included here was taken of him in The Street with his horse and cart.

There are photographs of two other carriers, George Batchelor shown with his cart.

Also Chris Mills, pictured with his daughter in the garden.

William Booker, a builder, was aged 20(?) when he bought in 1858 the stock of stone, slates tools and property of the late Thomas Caiger. Seven years earlier he was a bricklayer's labourer living with his father Thomas Booker, a widower, who worked as an agricultural labourer. From *Kelly's Post Office Directories* his progress can be traced.

1862 Stonemason

1867 Stonemason and builder

1874 Stonemason and builder

1878 Stonemason, builder and farmer

1887 Builder and contractor, undertaker, stone and general mason and dairy farmer.

His account books from 1856 show the work carried out, and his reputation as a builder was considerable as many of the large landowners in this area used him for work to their houses, outbuildings and cottages, and also he repaired most of the local churches. Other work included not only new houses, but buildings such as the Yapton School erected in 1861, and the Barnham Market as this developed through the 1890's.

There still exists a wages book, for 1888/93. The numbers working each week for this period fluctuated between 8 and 27. They worked a 10 hour day for six days a week, and the wages varied according to skills, the lowest paid being the labourers. Charles White a labourer was earning 9s..0d a week in April 1883, which was raised to 10s..0d in August and 11s.. 0d in April 1884. He was only paid for time worked, but did receive overtime. For that year his earnings averaged 10s..0d a week. By 1893 his wages had increased to £1..1..0 for a sixty hour week.

Pictured below is William Booker with his workmen outside the South Lodge of Avisford Park which was built for Colonel Henty in 1898 at a cost of £273. The old granary was taken down and the bricks, slates and timbers which were sound were used for this new lodge.

This photo of one of William Booker's employees, Charles White and his brother George was taken outside the thatched cottages on the corner of Tye Lane and The Street. George worked as a slaughterer for the butchers at the Humphrey Stores.

James Sparsholt also worked as a labourer for William Booker and then for his son Allan.

Two of William's sons Allan and Edward helped to develop the business and above is their headed note paper.

Below is a time sheet for one of their labourers.

TIME SHEET for the week ending *October 5th* 1895
of work done by *Funden* in the employ of
A. & E. BOOKER, Builders & Contractors, Walberton.

Mills and Millers

Walberton had two mills, a tower mill situated at the top of Mill Lane near the Green, and a post mill at Mill Road, Walberton Common (which is now part of Slindon). Both mills were demolished in 1898.

Charles Ayling wrote two interesting articles about the millers and mills, unfortunately undated.

"Our two jolly millers, being the stoutest and perhaps the richest men in the village are staunch Conservatives of course, at once the guiding spirits, and the guardian angels, of local Toryism . So staunch and true they are that once a year, on the 19th April, in a beautiful burst of political and poetical enthusiasm. they hang wreaths of primroses on each sweep of their wind mills to the 'Great Saint Ben'." [Disraeli]

The wind on Friday raved like a tempest out of temper and at times was a very good imitation of a downright hurricane. Our brave old windmill, after many a successful battle with the breeze and storm has got the worst of it now. One sweep is missing, and the vane or fan was also damaged. The old structure- quite a veteran among windmills — will have to take an autumn holiday and place itself under the 'doctors' hand. Matters have been worse and I can remember a storm in which all four sweeps came down with a smash, while the luckless 'fan' went spinning piecemeal over the fields." [This refers to the mill near the Green]

The two millers referred to in the first article were Solomon Short and Mark Luxford.

Solomon Short's mill, Mill Lane. Walberton Green.

*Mark Luxfords mill, Mill Road,
Walberton Common.*

Mrs Luxford, the Miller's wife

Game Keepers

Edward Baker was a gamekeeper living in west Walberton Lane according to the 1881 census. He was married and had five children living at home.

He is referred to in an article by Charles Ayling.

"With the gun — If our village sports men are good shots. they must have thinned out the partridges by this time. There has been a deal of powder expended among them. We know very little about pheasants, but walking through a cover one after-noon we came upon half-a-dozen fine 'long-tails,' with a curious white bird among them. It was not merely ringed or speckled, but almost if not entirely, white. Was it a 'sport' Mr Baker or an imported specimen? Can anyone tell us if partridges and pheasants are good to eat, and , if they are, who eats them all."

Mr Edward Baker, Gamekeeper.

*Mr Harry Moore, Gamekeeper, at his gate,
and again, below with vermin.*

Carpenters

The account books of two Walberton carpenters of the Victorian era still survive, giving details of the type of work they carried out and the amounts they charged. These books belonged to James Suter and William Sergant.

James Suter's work book is for the period 1851 to 1854. At the time of the 1851 census he was 55 years old, married and had two daughters living at home — Charlotte aged 17, a dressmaker and 14 year old Ann. James Suter's sister Mary, also a dressmaker, lived with them.

In 1851 he employed one man and sometimes he took on a labourer to help with the work. The type of work varied and the following is a sample with the prices charged.

	£	s	d
Repair gate at school house		1	3
Fixing coffee mill		1	3
Repairing chair and new bottom		8	
Coffin	1	15	0
Lining coffin		2	6
2 men half day putting up fence		6	4
Cutting oak trees		2	6
New carpet on gout stool		1	3
Sharpening saw			3
Taking down and putting up bedstead		2	6
Board for wagon		2	6
Mending drying rack		1	0
2 mop handles and broom handles		1	6
1/4 day on roof			9
Repairing granary tubs			9
New window frames and sashes		15	0
New coup for pheasants		7	0
Coffin for child		12	0

Several times by the amount paid were the words 'let off'.

William Sergant (1854-1934) was a carpenter and skilled woodsman and his wood and builder's yard was situated on The Street where Turnpike Garage is now.

In his day books, alongside the column showing work carried out, he often named the labourer employed. Some of the names mentioned were Blunden, Caiger, Palmer, Treagus, Batemen, J.B. Murell, C. White, and Denton Vinson.

Although William Sergant worked mainly in Walberton he did have clients in the surrounding villages. Extracts from his day book show who he worked for, the type of work, and the prices charged between 1894 and 1899.

	£	s	d
LADY ANSON			
Painting and varnishing croquet balls.		2	9
Repairing an old writing table and mending floor in maid's bedroom, fixing mirror over mantle in drawing room, and new line to sash in morning room.		7	9
MR J HUMPHRY			
Painting the Chapel outside	2	11	0
Mending two chairs, one elm, one walnut.		1	6

William Sergant, Carpenter, pictured here in Binsted woods.

Painting and papering both front rooms,
stair case, passages, one bedroom and all
outside work (materials £4..11..8, labour £10..1..0) 14 12 8

Repairing, painting and varnishing van. 4 14 4

MR W EWENS

Two mallets for breaking turnips for sheep 2 0

MR HATCHER

Building up inside of chimney, it caught fire
and came through under the floor upstairs
and was not safe to be left. 18 0

MR ELLIS

Putting in new grate in smoking room 1 9 6

Soldering refrigerator at the Brewery 3 6

Making bottle rack and repairing old one 3 1 5

MR S SHORT

Repairs at Mill Cottage, building up doorway
into store, taking out and building up at
bottom of Chapel stairs, boarding ceiling and
mending paper in places.

   Putting in new grate and white washing
ceiling of room in Shorts House. 8 18 11

MR H WHITEWICK

Making a door and frame for cottage 16 6

MR H HATCHER

One plough handle. 9

MR G BURCH (Thatcher)

New bucket and sucker to pump. 3 0

MISS BELL
Repairing wheels and break block of waggonette   1   2

WALBERTON SCHOOL MANAGERS
Cleaning out all earth closets at school and house.   1   6

CAPTAIN LONG, RN
Sweeping four chimneys, putting down carpets,
  hanging pictures and mending several pieces of
  furniture.   17   0

H HARTLEY
New steps in old bakehouse and making new
  doorway through floor of store to take flour
  in that way.   3   12   6

     William Sergant was also an undertaker, repairing and making headstones and coffins. The following gives a few details.

	£	s	d
Coffin for Henry Puttock's little girl, aged two days. (Yapton Lane) Paid sometime.		5	0
Headstone — Elizabeth Lucas, 88 years. 76 letters	4	5	0
Headstone — Elizabeth White. 117 letters	3	6	7
Coffin for Mary Ann Hatcher. Oiled elm with brass furniture. Two bearers 10/- Grave 7/6	3	12	6
Charlotte Smith, 35 years. 3/4 elm shell and one elm outside coffin. Polished with brass fittings.	15	14	7

     The following is a list of carpenters taken from Trade Directories published during the 19th century.

1832   James Lintott. Further entry for 1839.

1852   Charles Lintott. Further entry for 1858.

1832   James Suter. Further entries for 1839, 1852, 1858, 1862, 1867 and 1878.

1887   William Sergant — Carpenter and undertaker. Further entries for 1890, 1899 and 1903.

Denton Vinson, one of William Sergant's employees, seen here in Sergant's woodyard, on the site of what is now the Turnpike Garage, The Street, Walberton.

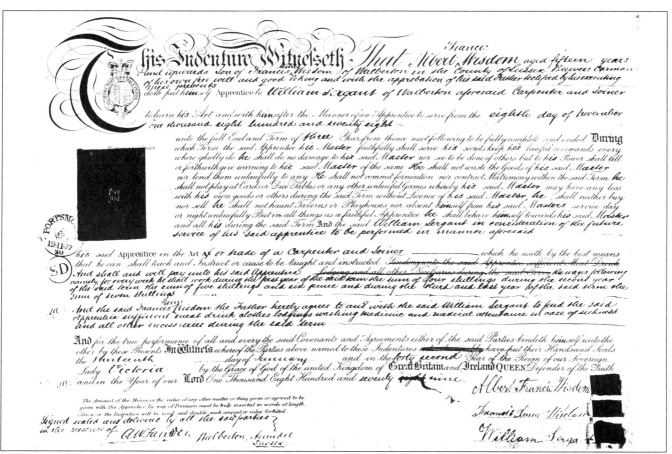

The Indenture of Albert Francis Wisdom, who was apprenticed to William Sergant when aged 15 in 1878.

Blacksmiths

There were two known working Smithy's in Walberton in the 19th century. There was one at Walberton Green, which was demolished a long time ago, and another at the corner of The Street and Yapton Lane, now known as Forge Cottages.

The Smithy at Walberton Green.

The names of the Blacksmiths in Victorian Walberton are taken from Trade Directories published during the 19th century.

1855 George Wakeford, Further entries in 1862 and 1887.

1852 Henry Hatcher. Further entry for 1862.

1867 Robert Hatcher.

1874 Mrs Mary Ann Hatcher. Further entry for 1878.

1887 Mrs Mary Ann Hatcher and Son.

1890 Harry Hatcher. further entries for 1890,1899 and 1903.

Harry Hatcher, who was known to be a blacksmith between 1887 and 1903.

Following Harry Hatcher's retirement, his premises were taken over by John Atkin who can be seen (below) at work in the forge.

In 1947 The Women's Institute produced a Village Scrap Book in which Mr Atkins, then seventy two years old, said of the art of the blacksmith:

"No other county in England can come up to Sussex's standard in this art, but it's finished now ... It's the machinery that's done it. It can't do it so well, but it does it cheaper."

Bakers

This list of Bakers is taken from Trade Directories published during the 19th century.

1832 James Gardner, miller and baker.

1832 John Randel, miller and baker. Further entry for 1839.

1839 Charles Gardner, miller and baker.

1839 Henry Farnden, baker. Further entries for 1852, 1858, 1862, 1867 and 1874.

1878 Elizabeth Farnden, baker.

1887 Harry Hartley, baker. Further entries for 1890, 1899 and 1903 mention him as baker and fruit grower.

Outside Hartley's bakery and grocery.

·BRENDA DIXON·

Harvest Notes

From the *West Sussex Gazette*, 19th September 1861.

Harvest rejoicings. The labourers from Tickner, Burtons and Suters farms were treated by their Masters. A booth was erected and Mrs Todman of the Royal Oak supplied good things and the band of the 9th Sussex Rifle Volunteers were present.

June 25th 1874

Preparing for harvest. In an empty barn by the Green some workmen are engaged preparing agricultural implements for harvest operations. Among other things they have put together a brand new reaping or mowing machine — we are not certain, which — not quite certain either if the two names don't mean the same thing. It is a curious complicated piece of machinery, strongly made and firmly knit together, but among heavy crops it must make hard work for the horses if not the machine. On board large steam boats they employ 'donkey engines' to do various work. Something of the kind ought to be invented to work this reaper, to spare the horses.

Harvest notes — 1880

While the steam thrasher is realising the results of the last harvest the steam plough is preparing for the next. This extensive use of machinery in our fields suggests some curious reflections. Twenty years ago, when steam was first pressed into the farmers service, exulting praises rang through the length and breadth of the land over the new era of prosperity and plenty that was to follow. Streams of cereal wealth and golden store were to make us all rich, contented, and happy. A glance around us, and another glance down the advertising columns of the *West Sussex Gazette* offers a striking commentary on those delightful vaticinations, for such a picture of ' depression' and ruin the agricultural world surely never offered, at least not in the present century.

August 1881

Harvest operations are not often carried on in such low temperatures. the evenings are quite chilly, and one day we saw men making an oat rick with their frocks and coats on, and small blame to them, for the wind was decidedly cold.

Machinery has cut the greater part of the corn this year. The curious clatter of the implement has been heard in all directions. and its odd movement — something like a miniature windmill — winding round the field, has attracted general notice. As a proof of its prevalent use, our village grocer, Mr Humphrey, who includes 'faghooks' in his very miscellaneous stock, tells us he has sold but one solitary implement this harvest, in place of five or six dozen — the average demand — in former years.

This mowing machine does a straight forward honest bit of work well and quickly, but if the straw does not stand upright, the machine makes rough work of it. Sometimes it won't cut it on any terms. Rabbits must consider themselves very badly treated animals, for looking on one evening as they were cutting a piece of oats we saw a bit of very animated sport — fun for all concerned except the rabbits. We forget how many were killed but only one escaped.

The photographs opposite were taken in 1901 of members of the Booker family working in a field off Tye Lane.

· BRENDA DIXON ·

Edward Booker,
mowing the hay.

Loading
the haycart

Itinerants

Charles Ayling writes:

"Every few months, Mr Farnden, whose farm fence abuts on the Green has to pay a man to repair it, and as it is repaired tramps and other itinerant make use of the material to boil their tea kettles and to cook their suppers. Only on Sunday week we saw three or four jolly looking roughs engaged in this pleasant occupation, in the freest, frankest manner possible, evidently thinking the material was put there for their own special convenience. We did not know then that some of the confounded fraternity had played us a similar trick, with worse results. They have not only torn away our fence, but carried off some wood that was inside of it, and so let the cows into the garden."

Rag and bone man, 1901 (above). Wicker-work hawker, 1902 (below).

Itinerant Gypsy, 1901

Harry Whitewick (above) with cow in the field opposite Pear Tree Cottages, and again (below) as a road sweeper.

Eliza Randall, whose father was a miller, was born in 1841, the youngest of five children. From the 1881 census we know that she worked as a needlewoman and lived with her mother, a 75 year old annuitant. This photograph was taken at the turn of the century when she was living in the bothy of Pear Tree Cottages, The Street.

Mr Bateman was the night watchman while the gas mains were being laid in 1901. He also sometimes worked for William Sergant.

Miss Anne Shipton, known locally as "Nanny Shipton", worked as a laundress and at the time of the 1881 census was 44 years old and lived at the east end of Pear Tree Cottages.

Laying the gas mains, 1901. This photo was taken from the bottom of Dairy Lane looking towards 'Dog Kennel Cottage' which was demolished in the 1920s and replaced with 'Kennel Croft'.

· BRENDA DIXON ·

Jassamine Cottage, The Street, 1901.

Miss Mary Ann Spiers lived in the bothy at the rear of this cottage. In 1881 she was aged 52 and was of independent means. These photographs were taken in 1900

Mr and Mrs Barnes, who lived in Barrack Row, 1901.

Mrs Eade, 1901

Mr Holden, 1901

Mrs Collins, 1901.

CRICKET

Walberton has for many years played cricket with varying degrees of success, and here are two matches which were lost recorded by the *West Sussex Gazette*.

17th June 1869 — Chichester verses Walberton. On Monday at Walberton the above clubs resulted in favour of Chichester.

July 31st 1892 — The return match between eleven boys of Walberton and eleven of Slindon was again crowned with success for the Slindonians.

From the *Walberton Almanack*, 1889:

The Cricket Club.

This has now become so well-established and on such a good foundation, that it must henceforth have a regular place in this little "Annual."

There are about thirty playing members. Seven matches were played last season, in three of which Walberton was victorious, and one match was "drawn." There were also two matches played between members of the Club, the Boys' match, and the Married and Single.

These matches involve very little expense to the players and the Club, being "Afternoon" matches, and so only light refreshments are needed.

The consequence is that three times as many matches can be played, and so a great deal more practice takes place. In fact every fine evening in the season play is going on.

The highest Batting and Bowling averages last season were made by Mr S Short, jun., and Mr G Tanner respectively. The

Walberton Cricket Club, c.1900.

Club is very much indebted to Mr Booker for the use of the best part of the May-pole field; to Colonel King for his generous support and active interest and to Mr Ellis for his services as Secretary and the good nature and patience with which he keeps everything going pleasantly."

1891 *Almanack:*

A great effort was made last summer on behalf of our Cricket Club, the result has been the erection of a very useful and convenient little Pavilion. So. you see. we are not standing still, even with respect to our amusements.

Mr Solomon Short jnr, c. 1900.

THE WALBERTON & YAPTON FLOWER SHOW

In 1856 Dr Vogan started the Walberton and Yapton flower, fruit and vegetable show and the *West Sussex Gazette* gave a report about this in the issue for 17th September 1860.

The Annual Exhibition by inhabitants of the parishes of Walberton and Yapton; took place last Thursday on the ground adjoining the vicarage in a large booth. The right wing for Walberton and the left for Yapton. The centre for choice flowers, exotics and floral designs.
Mr Blackmans brass band was in attendance, and dancing kept up the spirit despite the moist state of the turf. This the fourth annual exhibition, like its predecessors, passed off charmingly. At the conclusion three hearty cheers were given for our vicar and lady, the Rev and Mrs Vogan.

We know that this flower show was being held at the Vicarage Garden in 1867 as the *West Sussex Gazette* tells of how part of the Arundel Band was in attendance during the day and the evening finished with dancing.

Walberton and Yapton Flower Show 1866 (opposite)

A wave of cold
How terrible it was — that frigid wave,
Swiftly descending on the whirlwinds wing
Straight from the footstool of the great frost King!
Pallid as Death — relentless as the Grave —
Like an invading enemy it came,
Strong to destroy, with ruin armed and death —
A Hydra monster, slaying with its breath
And wreathing nature in a frozen flame!
On all things laid its petrifying vein!
Invisible, careering through the air,
With never a thought of mercy, or to spare,
The fiercest and the cruellest foe of man!
Alas! for earth — for all — when storm and tempest rolls,
If never a Power beyond directs it, or controls!

The church, seen from Dairy Lane, 1890s.

Passing Thoughts, Slindon Wood

I walked the other evening in a wood,
A noble beech wood, where the stately trees,
Like columns of a glorious temple, stood
Majestic, silent; not a passing breeze
Came to molest the leafy arch above;
Nor ev'n a song bird broke the stillness there,
Nor gambolling squirrels mid the branches move,
No humming insects stir the drowsy air.
'Twas strangely silent: man seemed far away,
And Nature slumbered, and the setting sun,
'Twixt the tall pillars, sent a parting ray
To warn the wanderer that his race was run
A golden glory seen, but when we seem
To catch a glimpse of heaven — in a dream.

AUGUST 1860

· BRENDA DIXON ·

Slindon wood, c. 1890

FROM 'THE WALBERTON ALMANACK'

A QUESTION FOR 1879
Would not a Parish Clock, in some central situation, be a very great convenience to all of us, and an ornament to our Village?

HINTS TO HOUSEHOLDERS.

To put out a chimney on fire — Throw on the grate a quantity of salt, and, if possible, stop the draught by nailing a wet blanket in front of the fire- place.

To extinguish paraffin oil — If your lamp falls and the oil ignites on the floor, the worst thing to do is to put water in it; the best extinguisher is earth, a few spadesful of which will put out the flames at once: but a mat, rug, blanket or cloth will do almost as well.

In case of your house taking fire — It may be well to remember that the nearest fire engines are at Arundel, Bognor, and Chichester.

Charles Burch (on the Green), undertakes to ride off for the Arundel engine, should a fire occur at night.

Appendices

APPENDIX A: Emigration Letters

October 31st 1831

Dear friend,

I have at last taken the opportunity to send you a few lines, stating my good health and happiness. I have wished a great many times that you had come with me. George and I left my brother in Quebec, the 3rd of August, and came to Pittesford to George's uncle, and I stayed there five days, and then I got work at a farmers near by, for eight dollars a month, and everything found but my clothes. We have got each of us a pair of boots, and we feel as happy as two lords. As for George he can just see out of his eyes he is so fat. James Shepherd, for all he was dreaming that he was going in some fairy country all the time- he paid his passage, bought his provisions — he sailed a week towards his fairy country as he said, and he was very sea-sick: and there was a pilot boat came near us, and he began to be sorry that he ever started, so he gave the pilot £8 to carry him to the Isle of Wight for poor old Walberton, and that pretty little girl, laid so heavy on his heart, that he would sink the ship if he had gone a little farther. I was very sea sick for three weeks myself, but I have been very well ever since. Please give my love to all my sisters, and tell George Southerton that I will treat him when he comes to America. If there is anybody that wishes to come to this country, tell them to be sure not to come to Quebec; they must come to New York. Be sure not to send any lazy folks, as this is no country for lazy folks; but for them that will work, this is a good country. They can get from 10 to 12 dollars a month in the summer. Bring clothing such as shirts, and cloth to make up after you get here, for the people wear their clothes different in this country: they wear no round frocks, nor breeches, they all wear coats and waistcoats like our English gentlemen. If you are afraid to bring your cloth unmade for fear of duty, you can turn down the edge of it, and baste it and then they cannot take it for duty. I shall be very glad to get a letter from you, for I long to hear from old England again. Jordan sends his best respects to you, and his love to his father and mother, sisters and brothers, and all enquiring friends. Dear friend, I hope you will send me a letter as soon as you can, direct it to me at Mr Aylings, Pittisford, Monro County, New York, America. So no more at present from your well wishing friend.

Mark Ruel.

To Mr William Christmas,
Walberton

Pittisford, August 23, 1831

Dear sister I now take the opportunity of sending a few lines to you, hoping it will find you in good health, as it leaves me at present, and in good spirits. We arrived at Quebec, 23rd of May, and we got the work first day, at the Cape: we worked till breakfast time, and then we quit. Then we went two miles back into the country, and then we went to work for a scotchman in his garden for three days, but he gives us nothing to eat but potatoes and milk, and a mess they make with the oatmeal, they call a stirabout, and we did not like it, we thought we had gone back to England again. We went back into the country about 12 miles, and there we got work for an Englishman, at 5 dollars a month, and then we thought we were well off, for we had our washing, boarding and lodging into the bargain. By that time I had a letter from my Uncle, and then we were persuaded to stay a month longer. We started from Quebec, and then we found my uncle, and his family, and they were very glad to see us. We got to uncle's the 18th August, there was only one man and me that came to Pittisford. We left James at Quebec: we was at uncle's five days and Mark got work near by uncles for 8 dollars a month, he might have got two dollars more, but he did not know the regular price till after he had agreed: he had his board, lodging and everything found but his clothes: Mark thinks of himself as well off as our Walberton Squire. I am living at my uncle's yet, and James is as happy as the King in London. George Wells and his wife left Quebec and went to Little York in Upper Canada, before we did. Mr Trew was a great friend to us at Quebec, but Mr —— was a great rogue: he tried to swindle us out of our money, but Mr Trew saw us righted . . .

Dear sister, I wish you were all here, and as well off as I am. Girls can have here one dollar a week or 10 shillings: a dollar is 8 shillings American money, and English money four and six pence. This is a very fine country, plenty of everything that is needful both for body and soul . . . The farmers had all done harvest, when we arrived; if we had got here before harvest we might have had from 12 to 14 dollars a month through the harvest and haying. We went one day with uncle and his family to a methodist camp meeting: there was a great many hundred people met together in the woods, a great distance from any house, where the methodists make a practice of going to serve the Lord in their way . . . Be sure if any of you comes not to come by the way of Quebec: be sure and come the way of New York,* for you will have a great way to travel from Quebec; any one can come here for 10 pounds . . . Bring all the money you can, for that is more use to you than anything else: you can get anything you want here for money. If you have not got any with you when you land, you can soon get work and get some . . . Give aunt's and uncle's love to all Worthing folks; and tell them that uncle says they are fools to stay there if they can't get a good living there, for they can here . . . So no more at present from your loving and affectionate brother,

George Jordan

*This advice is intended for those only who wish to come to the neighbourhood where the writer is settled.

Appendix B: List of Sources

SOURCES

Poems and articles throughout the book unless otherwise indicated are *West Sussex Gazette* newspaper cuttings, which are in a scrap book called "Passing Thoughts". At present this is in my possession but will be passed on to the West Sussex Record Office, Chichester.

Nearly all the photographs are from glass plates taken by Edward Humphrey of Walberton, and are now in the WSRO, Chichester, Neg Nos 4601–5001.

INTRODUCTION

"Charles Ayling, Photographer" from Kelly's Directory of Sussex 1862 and 1867, WSRO, Chichester.

The Walberton Almanack and Parish Register, WSRO, Chichester.

SETTING THE SCENE

Victorian County History, Sussex 11, page 217, WSRO, Chichester.

WALBERTON PARK AND AVISFORD PARK

Worthing Museum

Papers of the Stretfield family of Uckfield, East Sussex (supplied by John Eyre, Walberton)

Hawkins MS6[F1769], WSRO, Chichester.

MFSIFF 298–318, WSRO, Chichester.

EMIGRATION

MM12/1398:- Public Record Office, Kew.

Petworth Emigration Committee Minute Book: Petworth House Archives 138.

Log Book for the Ship "England", Petworth House Archives.

"Letters and Extracts of Letters from settlers at the Swan River, and in the United States, to their friends in the Western part of Sussex: Petworth House Archives 1070.

Quarter Session Returns with Analysis of Expenditure of poor Taxes for 1801-17: QCR/1/3/W1 (page 108), WSRO, Chichester.

Returns from Arundel and Bramber Rape 1826 on poor relief: QCR/1/3/W1 (page 109), WSRO, Chichester.

EDUCATION

Victoria County History of Sussex, Volume 2, page 439, WSRO, Chichester.

1841/MF/492 HO 107/1090, WSRO, Chichester.

Humphrey Collection, Walberton Almanack, WSRO, Chichester.

202/13/2/1, WSRO, Chichester.

E202/12/1, WSRO, Chichester.

1881 MF/666/RG11/125, WSRO, Chichester.

1851 MF, WSRO, Chichester.

1871 MF414 RG 10/1114, WSRO, Chichester.

EP1/22/2, WSRO, Chichester.

Letter in the possession of the family of the late David Humphrey.

Ed 121/17591, Public Record Office, Kew.

PUBS, BREWING & TEETOTALLERS

Arundel Petty Sessions Licensing Books, 1824–Aug 1876, WSRO, Chichester.

Arundel Quarter Sessions, Tradesmen, p.90

Kelly's Directories, Chichester Library.

ORTHODOX AND UNORTHODOX RELIGION

M1W/1/1/1,2,and 3, WSRO, Chichester.

M1W/1/3/1 to 5, WSRO, Chichester.

M1W/1/4/2, WSRO, Chichester.

PAR 202/8/1, WSRO, Chichester.

PAR 202/7/1, WSRO, Chichester.

EP1/222 1858, WSRO, Chichester.

Minute Book started in 1895 which was in the possession of Mr Geal, Pastor for Walberton Chapel.

WORK AND PLAY

Trade Directories, WSRO, Chichester.

Trade Directories, County Library, Chichester

Accounts Book, James Suter, Humphrey Collection, WSRO, Chichester.

Acounts Book, William Sargent, Brenda Dixon, Walberton.

John Booker, Walberton.

J.W. Burgess, Southsea.

APPENDIX C

Apart from the poems and articles on Walberton, Charles Ayling also wrote many items concerned with topics relating to the Victorian Era — several of them showing that little has changed in the intervening years in East–West relations. I am including here a small selection of these, but as some are very long, parts have been omitted.

WHAT NEWS?
From the East, what news?
Does the stubborn Turk refuse,
With courteous word, but kindling eye,
And half sarcastic smile. to bow,
At bidding of his old ally,
Before his mortal Muscov' foe?
And once again will his proud Navy ride,
In hostile pomp, the Euxine's stormy tide?
Is Sinope forgotten? Does he dare
To risk another Navarino there?
Is the "horsetail standard" loose? the flags unfurled?
The Cross and the Crescent to harass a world?

They tell us 'tis a goodly land
Where yet the Moslem walks as Lord,
And he who won it, sword in hand,
Has still his hand upon the sword,

And stands prepared to lift again
His fearless war note's loud refrain.
Allah il Allah — 'tis the noble cry
Of men that will be victors, or will die,
Allah il Allah — God alone is great,
The one supreme sole arbiter of fate.
And for this creed, his fearless faith,
The Turk will die, and smile in death.

They tell us 'tis a glorious land,
The Bosphorus layes on either hand;
A land so bright, a realm so fair,
As war had never wasted there,
Though seldom has it smiled in peace
Since Jason sought the Golden Fleece.
And for a land so fair,
So robed in living light,
Shall the restless Russian bear,
And the Moslem mastiff fight?
And scratch and rend and tear
In shuddering Europe's sight?
No lifted hand the strife to stay,
None to forbid the barbarous fray.

Has Bruin set out on his march to the south
To snatch up the infidel dog in his mouth?
To shake him and cuff him and give him a kick.
And tell him he is so confoundedly "sick,"
Such a low, mangy brute, in such pitiful plight,
That the bestway to cure is to kill him outright.

What went ye out to see?
Ye wise ones of the West.
Would our own England bend the knee
With the swordpoint at her breast?
And did ye sagely think to find
In yonder wild Turanian brood
A warrior race of milder mind?
The Moslem of a milder mood
Could haughty Islam on her knees,
With low salaam and humble thanks,
Blow her own brains out just to please
Her Christian brother on the Neva's banks?

Let Europe frown with anger, blush for shame,
Or smile with mixed amusement and regret,
The Turk has won the diplomatic game,
And made of each wise "plenipo" a bête.*

*This word – a favorite one with our French neighbours.

WAR – THE BURNT VILLAGE

War, with its fiery breath, had passed
And left a seared and desolated land:
Burnt, blackened ruins; harvests half unripe
And half unreaped, ungathered in the fields.
All ruined, trampled, trodden under feet
Of myriads armed, commissioned to destroy:
Terror before them, famine fast behind,
And fiery plague and pestilence and death.

See that poor peasant peering from the woods,
Doubtful and trembling; e'en the falling leaf
Affrights him, and in every quiv'ring reed,
By fear and fancy magnified, he sees
The dreaded Uhlan with his pennoned spear.

Where shall he find the pleasant home he left
But yester evening, when the gathering roar
Of battle drove him to the forest shades,
With all his trembling little ones around him?

And is this all the passing foe has left
Of twice three hundred houses – – once a street
Of bright and cheeerful habitants? Behold
At either end a single house untouched,
And all the rest in ashes!
"This is war,"
Poor Jacques may cry, "and I am ruined now."

15th December 1870

FROM THE EAST

The moaning eastwind brings a bitter cry:
Can ye not hear it on the evening air?
That long, sad wail of anguish and despair
From myriads doomed to suffer — some to die.
They little ask, and find it not; the sky
is brass above them, and the earth beneath,
As the scorched ashes of a furnance, dry —
Yields one grim crop of misery and death.
Alike the early and the latter rain
Fails to descend to fertilise the soil,
And anxious millions watch the clouds in vain —
Fate hands them o'er to Famine for a spoil.
All hearts are failing, trembling, and afraid.
Heaven help them now, and England, too, will aid.

They hear her name with wonder and with awe —
(They fought her legions, impotently brave) —
Her queen their mistress, and her will their law.
They own her power, and cry to her to save:
Nor vainly cry, for England wages there
A strife unwonted in the march of Time,
A noble war with Famine and Despair,
With adverse Nature for a foe sublime —
A fearful foe to battle with. The eye
Looks on in wonder at the awful strife,
In which the prize of victory is the life
Of teeming millions.
They must live or die;
As Norhbrook wins or loses in the fight,
A sad, a novel, yet a noble sight.

I have seen it stated somewhere that a Bengalee laborer will live well on 18 or 20 annas — about 9d or 10d — a week. It seems strange and hard that such a people should perish for want of food.

JUBILEE IN THE EAST — Last week we had the pleasant privilege of listening while a young lady read a most interesting manuscript letter, giving a description of Jubilee rejoicings in Her Majesty's Indian Empire. Those rejoicings are already past, climatic reasons making it desirable that it should come off in February instead of June. The whole Indian Empire seems to have come out in one general burst of rejoicing over the unwonted event. The illuminations and fireworks, in both of which the oriental races take great delight, were so magnificent that England will have to do its "level best," as the Americans would say, not to be outshone and outdone in those two departments. The present state of affairs in India is very gratifying to English feeling, and specialy so when we reflect that less than 30 years ago the whole of that magnificent empire was all but torn from her grasp in that fearful outburst, prompted alas, chiefly by "the wild justice of revenge" for years of opppression and misrule. The Indian Mutiny of 1858 was an awful business, but, like an atmospheric tempest, it cleared the air, and it also cleared the country of "John Company," and his avaricious hordes, who were kicked out, but not half so ignominiously as they deserved. Since the Queen and her Government assumed full control of Indian affairs, the people have been ruled chiefly with an eye to the people's good, and the result is they are prosperous, contented, and happy. A pleasant picture for an English eye.

· BRENDA DIXON ·